UNARMED GARDENING

UNARMED GARDENING

How to Tame the Thing Outside

**FRANK WARD
AND
WILLIAM RUSHTON**

Macdonald General Books

Macdonald & Jane's * *London & Sydney*

© William Rushton/Frank Ward

First published in 1979 by Macdonald and Jane's Publishers Ltd, Paulton House,
8 Shepherdess Walk, London N1 7LW

ISBN 0354 08554 9

Designed by David Fordham

Typeset in Great Britain by C. Leggett & Son Ltd, Mitcham, Surrey

Printed and bound in Great Britain by William Clowes & Sons Ltd, Beccles, Suffolk

Contents

Acknowledgements

The authors wish to thank the following for their assistance in bringing *Unarmed Gardening* to fruition. Geoff Hamilton, editor of *Practical Gardening*, for his technical second opinion and one Senior Service cigarette; Diane Stanford for retyping a scruffy manuscript and laughing in all the right places; Tropical Greenhouses, Canklow Meadows, West Bautry Road, Rotherham, South Yorkshire, for a foolproof way of assembling a greenhouse; Florada Garden Products, Dollar Street House, Dollar Street, Cirencester, for bringing a new dimension to conservatory styling and construction; Charcon Products Ltd, Hulland Ward, Derby, for their Derbyshire paving/walling range which cuts in the right place; Stapeley Water Gardens Ltd, London Road, Stapeley, Nantwich, Cheshire, for making aquatic gardening so easy to dive into; Emess Lighting, Station Estate, Eastwood Close, London, for making midnight weeding possible; Ken Muir, Honeypot Farm, Weeley Heath, Clacton-on-Sea, Essex, for helping strawberries to grow vertically.

The publishers would like to thank Carters Tested Seeds Ltd for permission to use a seed packet for jacket photography.

Introduction

Do you have areas of waste land at the front and back of your house? Are they inhospitable regions, only to be traversed as an act of daring? Are they subject to open derision and private petitions by neighbours? Does the thought of reclamation ever cross your mind? Would you like a garden without the constant effort?

Answer 'Yes' to any of these questions, and if you have any sort of conscience at all, this book is the first step to a new peace of mind.

There are said to be fourteen million gardeners in Britain. Translated, this means 'There are fourteen million people in Britain with gardens'. Possessing a garden and being a gardener are two entirely different attributes. You, with scant interest and limited knowledge, are in the numerically superior 'people with gardens' section.

It isn't much fun being labelled a social outcast and a domestic layabout because of the state of the thing outside. Who wouldn't occasionally swap the cheese sandwich in front of the box for a modest barbecued sausage or two, cooked in real air; or the tin of mushy carrots for a handful of fresh orange roots, plucked long before their prime?

All this, and more, can be yours with as much or as little effort as you wish. The object of this book is to advise on how best to avoid gardening, and yet miraculously boast a garden that implies a skill and enthusiasm way beyond actual levels. The method requires some initial energy, and varying amounts of cash according to ambition, but everything described is perfectly attainable.

An example: weeds are one of the great wonders of this planet. You will be well aware of their ability to grow anywhere, any time, and to the most marvellous proportions – without the slightest assistance, and despite vicious, if sporadic, assaults. Happily there are numerous domesticated plants – with flowers too! – that share the same ability to thrive whatever you do, or don't do, to them. These we shall call The Survivors, a priceless blessing to the pseudo gardener. We shall deal with them fully later on.

There are few more effective labour-saving gardening methods than covering up the earth altogether. Don't be frightened by visions of the notorious green-painted concrete; means do exist to construct a tasteful concrete garden abundant in living, fragrant

This is the last time
I try to cross-fertilise
the Triffids

The Authors seen here conferring with their Editor, while in the background a companion strangles water-vole

things, the envy of all who see it. And if you spend much more than a couple of hours a year on it, you're overworking. The secrets of this ultimate solution are revealed in The Concrete Bit, a mouth-watering section which also embraces the essential horticultural basics of mixing cement, brick laying and paving. Anyone can do these things to a fairly professional standard; it takes the amateur a bit longer, that's all.

So far, all this is really relevant to the total leisure garden. It may be that you actually want to devote part of the diminishing space to growing food. Again, that process is ridiculously simple, assuming, as we must, that whatever comes up is a bonus. Most gardening literature concentrates on growing bigger and better vegetables and fruit, with the consequent encroachment on available time to spend just sitting and looking at your handiwork. We shall not be suggesting that sort of super-enthusiasm here. We'll tell you when and how, and perhaps throw in a few optional extras, but our veg look after themselves.

All gardens have their share of the corporately termed 'pests and diseases'. This unsavoury grouping embraces everything from slugs to greenfly, from mildew to peach leaf curl. These are sent to plague the keen gardener in particular, because naturally the more plants you have, the greater range and variety of pests and diseases you can accommodate. Unjust as it may seem, we can expect to attract less attention through disinterest. Nevertheless, there is bound to be the odd, less-discriminating bug or pestilence. Some are not worth bothering with. Others will, unfortunately, require identification and a squirt from one of the many, ready-mixed deterrents available. It can be quite good fun.

Having grasped the noble purpose of the work, we can now anticipate learning the ignoble skills to achieve it. 'Laziness is nothing if not well carried out' a matchbox once said.

1. The Thing Outside

Let us take a leisurely look at the thing outside, and consider the implications of it. Sizes vary tremendously, but we can safely assume that it is largely untamed, snarls when you appear and has a generally sullen nature. This kind of resentment tends to be the result of neglect or misunderstanding. The thing will only behave once you have come to terms with the problem and resolved to tame it once and for all. You might even come to care for it.

Like giving up smoking or going on a diet, the task ahead requires the right frame of mind. Summon up all reserves of willpower and determination. Once sufficiently braced, that is the time to move in with a fair degree of confidence. It can be a great shock to the system, but this will pass as conditions start to improve. And any regrets are more than compensated for by the diminishing guilt feeling.

The chances are that you have two things – one at the back and a smaller one at the front. Perhaps even a bit on the side. Decide which one you will have a go at first. This might be the front, because it's mostly smaller, more exposed to public scrutiny and therefore the main target for amusement and gossip.

Without doubt, this area in front of your house should be the first candidate for the ultimate in labour-saving methods. Unless you are exceptionally gregarious, the front thing is not the place for idling away leisure hours, nor is it a suitable venue for growing vegetables. No, this will be our showpiece, gracing your home and improving the whole image of the street in which you live.

It is fair to say that the non-gardener can achieve acclaim by being different. Labour-saving gardens tend to be out of the ordinary, and this very asset can hide a multitude of sins and motives. Being different in the gardening sense often implies greater enthusiasm, not less. The reconstructed plot is seen for what it is, and not for the purpose for which it was created. Such reasoning is particularly valid when it comes to concrete gardening; and concrete gardening is particularly suitable for front things.

ROUND THE BACK

The back thing, on the other hand, is very much more flexible and has a whole new set of considerations. We will assume that it is the larger of the two problems, more private, and where any wasting will be done. Concrete, green and vegetable bits can be amalgamated here in varying ratios according to choice, money or lethargy.

Inevitable failures in growing things can be discreetly hidden at the back, and will in no way feature prominently against the other things we shall talk of that 'you can't go wrong with'. Here, too, can be erected that great British garden edifice – The Shed. Where would we be without sheds? For a start, even fewer garages than at present would be used actually for putting cars in, and a vast proportion of the country's spider population would be homeless. Sheds are OK, and they cover up ground, too.

While on this subject, it is impossible not to draw your attention to the customised allotment shed. While not recommending them for the garden, allotment sheds are masterpieces of re-cycling, comprising just about all known materials and as such are as much an expression of their builder as any surrealist canvas. (And you don't have to wait for someone to tell you what it is.)

However, just as cryptic art needs an explanation to avoid wrong guesses, so the decision on what type of garden you require demands careful consideration if you and it are going to achieve harmony.

Older gardens are, on the whole, easier to deal with than new ones freshly vacated by the builder. The older garden, though disgracefully untidy and time-consuming, may well incorporate certain features worth keeping and thereby reduce the amount of reshaping to be done. A modest tree or two is always a nice start, particularly if they are evergreen and don't litter the place up every autumn.

The general rule is that if your garden is established, up to a point, adapt it to become more self-sufficient, rather than churn the lot up and start again. This does not, of course, apply to the old, established collection of all known weeds. Anyone attempting to justify a lessening of horticultural effort on these grounds is either beyond hope or a botanist.

New gardens, ravaged by excavations for rising mains and enriched by enough half-buried material to start a second house, are slightly more of a problem. What generally happens is that the garden is effectively turned upside down – clogging sub-soil from foundation work and the like is dumped on the top-soil. There are compensations, even so, and a few lorry-loads of fresh top-soil can cover all sorts of things. And, also important, there's the opportunity to start from scratch with a master plan for long-term energy conservation, unhindered by existing monsters like straight concrete paths built to withstand any conventional assault tool.

Almost any type of land can be converted, so don't be deterred by the present mess or seemingly insurmountable geological problems. Naturally sloping land is great for gardens, and quite considerable amounts of rubble can be usefully employed in our small scale construction work, much of which will be done with the proverbial knife and fork. The secret is always to use what's there as far as possible; after all it's much easier than fighting against it.

WHAT TYPE ARE YOU?

At this point, it is worth performing a little honest soul searching to establish exactly what type of 'thing victim' you are. Is it that you just don't have enough time (we're being honest, remember!)? Don't like it? Hate it? Or will devise any excuse to avoid expending one erg of energy in the immediate outdoors?

Perhaps shortage of time, either through the demands of your job or other pressing interest, is your reason/excuse. If so, it is *just* possible that a grain of enthusiasm might be lurking within. In this case it is worth considering a slightly more adventurous garden that requires you to lift more than one finger at a time. This latent curiosity, though ruthlessly suppressed, might yet flourish – in a small way – once initial apprehension has been dispelled. The time that seemed to be absent could suddenly be available in sufficient quantity to grow a radish, or even two.

If, on the other hand, the torment of self-analysis has positioned you in one of the other three categories mentioned above, it would be wiser to pursue an easier route to

gardening tranquillity. By adopting some of the tactics described later, even the most ardent opponent of cultivated plant life can make a bee's day.

Sadly, this wondrous contribution to Nature's bounty cannot be attained without an initial sacrifice. (This does not mean ritually slaughtering the neighbour's cat, even if it does deserve it.) The sacrifice demanded is one of physical effort and financial commitment. While certainly more distasteful than a simple offering, such rigours must at all times be viewed as *an investment for future laziness.*

The more inactive you intend to be in the long term, the more active you must be in the short term: such is the way of things. But equally inescapable is the comparison we might draw from a fundamental law of physics – energy can be changed, but none of it is lost. It is to be hoped, therefore, that the energy we commit to creating an idler's paradise will be repaid many times over with the aid of a few supercharging devices.

In any case, it would be premature at this stage to start getting depressed about the task ahead. We are not, after all, going to landscape a park or build a cathedral – just tame that irritating space near the house.

Further consolation can be gained from the strategy of 'doing it in stages'. Apart from self-inflicted injury, this is perhaps the most believable of delaying tactics. So much can be said in support of such an approach, much of it true, that it will invariably find sympathetic ears. Who could disregard the caution of the untutored who merely wanted to make sure he had performed the best possible job by carefully considering each step? No, you're on to a winner with this one; I can hear the violins playing now.

Such concern for quality tends to present itself frequently when you are actually engaged in the work. There's an irresistible temptation to stop and admire each brick painstakingly located into a new wall, or every super-resistant plant clumsily plunged into the ground. These are moments to relish, in which you can marvel at your own unprecedented skill, and instantly detect the vast difference each component makes. Such subtle changes are only appreciated by the

creator, however, so don't waste time getting the rest of the family to see and express their astonishment every five minutes. They won't understand. How could they?

It is just possible that you might persuade one or more of the household complement to help you. But beware of fickle labour. A rush of offers out of spontaneous enthusiasm can lead to you being left with all the grotty jobs; give them all the grotty jobs and you'll be back on your own inside half-an-hour. All this is particularly true of juvenile assistance – who *needs* someone to make patterns in cement, or introduce caterpillars, specially imported from friends' gardens, to new food supplies?

You can, of course, pay for specific duties. But gone are the days when a whole Scout troop could be hired for a pound a shift; and even those closest and dearest are not unaware of the quick killing to be made on a job you're trying with all subtlety to avoid. At least the promised transfer of currency provides sufficient incentive to ensure completion, and a small audience for your more artistic endeavours.

CHECK THE FUNDS
Bribery brings us to the next vital factor that must be taken into account before deciding on the new form your garden(s) will take. Money.

The manageable garden can be produced quite cheaply, but for the ultimate in conservation of time it will be necessary to increase funding considerably. Doing it yourself brings the master project within bounds, and the cost of materials is then the only remaining restriction. We shall talk later of economies that can be made, but if you really want to sit around and do nothing for 99.9 per cent of the year and still have a garden that looks great all the time, then for most of us there's no other way to achieve this than by spending money.

Against this theory, consider how much you might save by slaving over a very productive garden – and then compare the amount with how much you might earn grasping in the same length of time. The results are often surprising, and many a

money-saving fallacy has been destroyed in this way. The only real reason for total gardening is enjoyment, and at this stage of the proceedings that is one compensation not applicable to us.

Financial considerations will largely determine the material part of your garden, but not the general concept. Just remember that paving is more expensive than grass, walls cost more than fences or hedges, hardy plants that keep their leaves and colour all year round are priced higher than ones that have only a short life span. Generally then, if it's going to last longer and need less attention, it costs a lot more initially but should pay for itself in the long run. I know. I've seen the washing-up liquid commercials to prove it.

However, as has been said before, the garden can be a mixture of horticultural restraint at various levels. While the thought of a patio extending from the house to all boundaries north, south, east and west makes your mouth water, economics can make it very difficult to achieve in an effective way.

Ponder all the foregoing points as background information. We shall be dealing with many of them in detail and it helps, when coming to a 'physical' section, to be

acclimatised, at least partially. Early determination to crack the current problem is ideal, but resignation will do.

Fortify yourself with the knowledge that while that thing outside may appear to have a will of its own, it is in truth a medium for vegetative growth that, as far as we are concerned, doesn't have the sense to know what it should encourage and what it shouldn't, when left unattended. This statement is an affront to Nature's impeccable taste and selection. But we are the odd ones out in wanting, and being able, to change things artificially; and there's hardly a food crop or a popular flower grown that hasn't been engineered to its present state by man.

On this basis we justify our humble attempts to engineer a subdued garden. Within a few generations it might become feasible to control the weather, or at least predict it accurately, so that the unarmed gardener can make fuller use of his leisure, unshielded from the atmosphere and its perverse mechanics.

Only the enthusiast will philosophically gaze out at torrential weekend rain and contribute the immortal phrase 'Well, it will do the garden good'. Involuntary watering at peak relaxation hours gets right up my nose.

2. Escape Routes

Introduction

Those of you who have seen wartime prison escape dramas will be fully familiar with the imaginative methods employed to disappear from one side of a barbed wire fence and reappear on the other undetected. To a degree, such stirring acts are an inspiration for this section of *Unarmed Gardening*, though it is only fair to point out the impracticability of disposing of a garden by trickling it out of the bottom of your trouser legs. One or two may actually have got there like that.

Our escape routes are far less daring, but do embrace a certain cunning, entering into the spirit of evasion at its most honourable level. The techniques are perfectly legitimate, aimed totally at saving time and energy – spiced with a touch of honest desperation.

Escape will be made by four complementary operations. First comes the Plotting. At this stage the plans are laid, utilising basic principles of design as a foundation for all that will follow. It's a vital phase, fundamental to successful absconding, and must encompass the approach to any natural obstacles, unnatural obstacles, and alternative plans, as well as startling the intellect with a spot of primitive geometry.

Next comes the Cover Up. Here we consider the best ways of disguising gardening ineptitude or reluctance by applying a manageable surface to the rampant soil below. These include the maximum security of paving or concrete, and semi-permanences such as gravel, lawns and other mass ground cover. This is a significant section, showing some light at the end of the tunnel, so to speak.

Thirdly, we enlist the support of the non-gardener's best friends – the Survivors. These are tough, botanical allies that can take on weeds at their own game, thriving on abuse, withstanding criminal neglect, and looking as well-cared for as the average radiant dandelion that never enjoyed a stroke of assistance in its life. Without such crucial aid the chances of escape would diminish greatly.

Lastly, we look at the help that Tools can give us. Ever since early man discovered that a sharp stone worked better on his Sunday mammoth joint than merely tearing it apart by hand, the introduction of a tool has made one job after another that much easier. (What he could have done with a power saw is nobody's business – there would have been a lot of three-legged mammoths for a start.) We have numerous mechanical aids for attacking gardens, from flame-throwers to self-propelled sprinklers. Some of them we shall be pleased to own.

Together, these four primary subjects provide the answer to our present problem. We go on to look at each one in more detail now before branching out into the actual task of construction that will make the dream of freedom a reality.

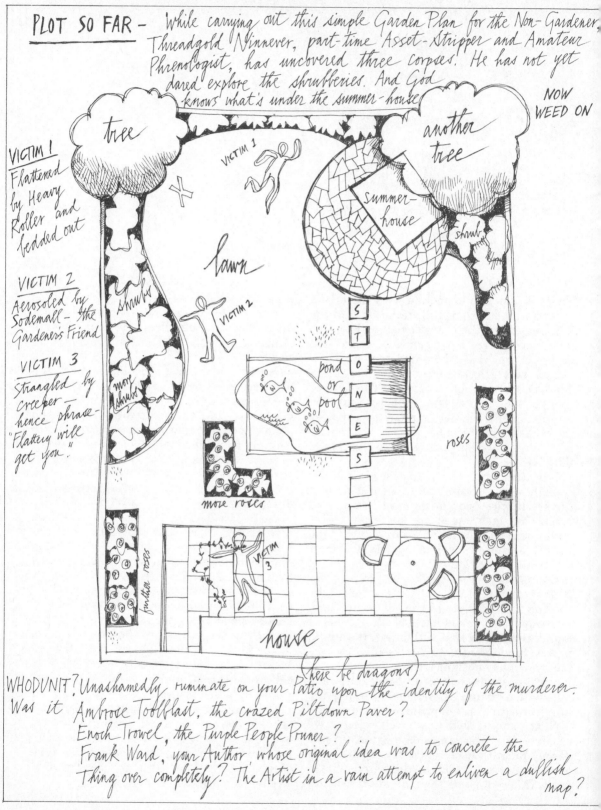

PLOT SO FAR — While carrying out this simple Garden Plan for the Non-Gardener, Threadgold Ninnever, part-time Asset-Stripper and Amateur Phrenologist, has uncovered three corpses. He has not yet dared explore the shrubberies. And God knows what's under the summer-house

NOW WEED ON

tree

another tree

VICTIM 1

summer-house

shrub

VICTIM 1
Flattened by Heavy Roller and bedded out

VICTIM 2
Aerosoled by Sodemall — the Gardener's Friend

VICTIM 3
Strangled by creeper — hence phrase — "Flattery will get you."

lawn

shrubs

more shrubs

VICTIM 2

S
T
O
N
E
S

pond or pool

roses

more roses

further roses

VICTIM 3

house
(here be dragons)

WHODUNIT? Unashamedly ruminate on your Patio upon the identity of the murderer. Was it Ambrose Toolblast, the crazed Piltdown Paver?
Enoch Trowel, the Purple People Pruner?
Frank Ward, your Author, whose original idea was to concrete the Thing over completely? The Artist in a vain attempt to enliven a dullish map?

2. Escape Routes Plotting

Plotting, or design, of a garden is often a compromise between what you would ideally like and what you can realistically achieve or afford. But a little fantasy at the pencil and paper stage costs nothing, and the most ambitious plan can subsequently be reduced in grandeur until it comes into financial focus. None of my great masterpieces have yet passed the bank account test, so we shan't give them space here.

You'll be pleased to know that a fair bit of time should be spent doodling. This is legitimate armchair activity. Being creative, it is also a great strain on the mind, justifying regular refreshment, release from other duties etc. (I knew you'd like it.)

What you need is some scrap paper or a notepad on which to draw a rough outline of the garden. Position any existing features and then start to map out possible shapes of patios, lawns, flower beds, vegetable patch etc. You might do dozens before settling on the bird's eye view that appeals to you most.

At all times consider the fundamental ease of maintenance, and how the garden will be used in practice. It's not easy when contemplating the ultimate in design to concern yourself with such mundane problems as where's the dustbin going to be, or where do we hang out the washing? Such items must be considered, of course, and careful provision made for their discreet siting.

'Ideas will come as you start to tackle each section' is a comforting phrase applied to anything that demands a degree of original thought. A much better way is to pinch other people's ideas. This happens all the time, and what's wrong with incorporating the best features of the opposition into your own product anyway?

Professionals describe this as being 'influenced' by so-and-so's work. The best way to be influenced is to look into other people's gardens for features that you might copy or adapt. It is not always easy to view a good range of designs, unless your job takes you regularly within spying distance; and a more than casual interest in a strange garden can alarm its owners, particularly if you start making notes. So be discreet.

Assuming you have some initial thoughts on things you would like to incorporate, we can now return to the drawing board and run through a few basic guidelines.

GENERAL

First decide exactly what you want from your garden and what type of use it will get. We know it needs to be easy to maintain, but if you have very young children should you have a pool? Will the garden be used as a play area and therefore need to be highly durable? Is it big enough to embrace all the chosen features without looking cluttered? Your terms of reference are as much a restriction as a guide.

There is much to be said for the simple approach. While archways and bridges look great, it is of little use building them in if they are unlikely ever to be completed. Consider, too, the maintenance of any exotic features, because the whole point of the exercise is to minimise effort in the interests of gardening celibacy. For example, remember that decorative wooden ornaments will need regular treatments with preservative to keep them in good condition and prevent rotting.

Don't commit the great classic of siting your prime relaxation area in eternal shade. The amount of sun any part of your garden gets will play a large part in deciding where certain things appear. This can be a problem in some gardens that receive very little sun except in the most exposed quarters. You have to decide if the sunniest spot can be screened for privacy; if not, then it's a case of working backwards to the first available area. Unless absolutely ideally suited, you will have to follow the sun around in any case – so as far as possible keep a good section of the arc clear of buildings, borders, veg patches and so on. Who wants the sunniest garage in town?

Take a lesson from some town planners, who manage to contrive maze-like approaches to some key services such as bus stops, telephone booths and pillar boxes. How often have you stood ten yards from such a facility and had to walk fifty yards to reach it? That's the surest way of getting those shrub borders trampled, or sections of grass worn to a naked trail. Direct routes are a key feature of planning, and if they don't exist they'll soon be made. Think of this when linking regularly visited parts of the garden.

HEAPS FILL HOLES

If you have a load of rubble – one of the unnatural obstacles from which escape is necessary – consider ways in which it can be used and therefore disposed of. Patios, paths, and walls all need a hardcore base, so these are obvious solutions. Bits of old iron and the like can also go into foundation work, forming an excellent reinforcement. Raised sections can use up even more rubbish and a variety of elevations adds considerable interest to a garden without a great deal of effort. Consider such techniques as killing two birds with one bit of rubble. If all else fails, the only answer is to hire a skip – you'll find the details in your Yellow Pages or local newspaper.

Ponder the order in which things will be executed. Any excavation work should be done first, and this inevitably produces a heap equivalent to the hole. If your plan requires excavation it ought, in the interests of containment, also to include an area or areas of elevation. If not you will be left with a disposal problem, unless everything can be spread evenly over the remaining area. Even so, this is not good practice as we don't particularly want sub-soil appearing at the top, do we?

As your paperwork plan develops, try to imagine it in the three-dimensional sense. Ground plans are OK, but do leave a lot to the imagination. Heights are just as important as surface areas, so when marking in a wall get an idea of how high it should be and, in the case of ornamental screens within the garden perimeters, the general rule is 'low enough to see over – high enough to avoid tripping over'.

GRASS

Grassed areas in the shape of lawns must be easy to cut, otherwise just having one is going to create a lot of unnecessary work. Things to remember when planning a lawn are that it should be slightly higher than any adjoining paths and should not go right up to walls. The reason for this is that you will find it impossible otherwise to mow right up to the edges, and then you'll have to grovel around with a pair of shears to finish the job. Just

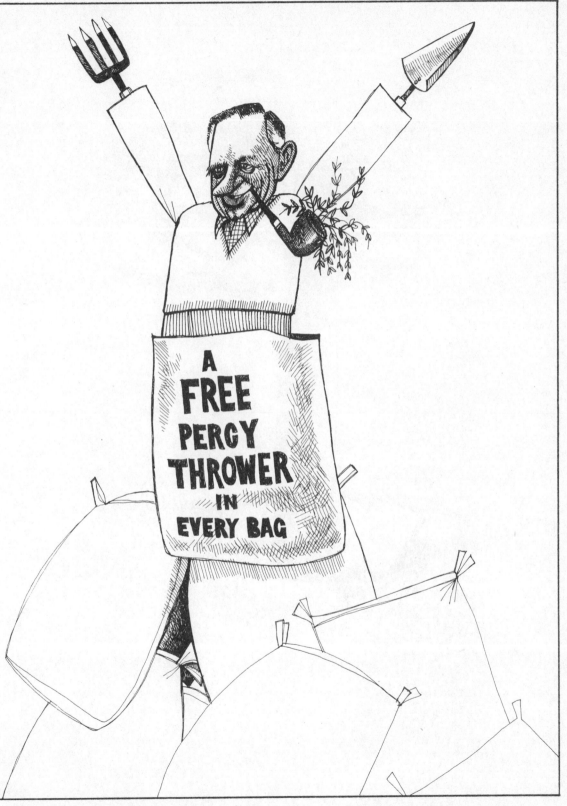

this sort of oversight can cause grassphobia, the fear of cutting lawns – a dreadful affliction. Particularly for lawns.

Think twice before creating grassy slopes, which certainly look attractive but have to be cut, and that means an uphill struggle. And remember that each time you stick a flower bed in the lawn you are creating more edges to trim.

If you have, or plan to include, a tree within the lawn, a small circle around the base of the trunk could be surfaced with stone to make mowing around the obstacle easy.

When deciding on a shape, it is worth noting that in small gardens, large sweeping curves give an impression of space. This might be a little frightening in making you think there's more garden there than you at first imagined, but I throw in the observation for what it's worth.

If by some misfortune, accident, carelessness, or divine punishment, you, as a non-gardener, have a really large garden by the tail, then grass might be an aid to escape. A large proportion of the area can be set aside for an orchard and covered in coarse grass. You'll have to get a power mower but generally the space can look like a field and get away with it. And you will have provided a good spot for the kids to play in too.

TREES
The main thing to remember about trees is the old saying 'From little acorns giant oak trees grow', taken at its most literal. While none of us are likely to be inconvenienced by the mature product of an acorn planted now, the ultimate size of trees must be considered when siting them. A flowering almond I brought home in my car seven years ago now wouldn't do me a lot of good if I ran into it. Have a tree or two by all means, but don't go mad in a small garden – and don't plant one too close to the house. (It will eventually stop a lot of light, and root systems are often bigger than the exposed branches.)

There are, as you know, trees that keep their leaves (known as evergreens) and trees that shed them every autumn (deciduous). It must be a point to consider, conserving energy (ours) as we are, that evergreens are

our best bet, being a lot less messy. Go to your local garden centre to study the range of trees available. Of all the evergreens, conifers are certainly the most popular.

BEDS
When planning beds for shrubs, flowers or whatever, consider the possibility of raising them. The raised bed adds interest, reduces the amount of bending to be done, and provides an opportunity for a nice bit of walling. Don't raise beds against fences because you'll (a) rot the woodwork and (b) put excessive weight on the lower part of the structure. Small amounts of raising, say up to six inches, are possible, but the affected part of the fence must first be lined with corrugated asbestos or PVC sheeting.

PATIOS
In the interests of labour saving, patios should be as large as you can afford. A patio should not be considered as a barren expanse of paving or concrete. It can be on more than one level, embrace raised flower beds and/or an ornamental pool, as well as having spaces left for plants. Remember, too, that stocked containers can be stood on the patio and moved around to vary the appearance.

Patios logically appear next to the house, but there is no reason why a secondary paved area should not be included in the design at another part of the garden or, indeed, in the case of a small plot, why the entire space should not be based on paving. The small front garden is a natural for this approach.

PATHS
Paths should generally be as wide as possible, as should any steps that may be needed in sloping ground. Narrow routes give the garden a feeling of restriction and walking them starts to demand concentration. The conscious struggle to master pedestrianism is best left behind at around twelve months old, to be revived only in the event of alcoholic over-indulgence. Narrow paths make the manoeuvring of vehicles, such as wheelbarrows, much more difficult, as well.

The point about width also applies if you are intending to make a drive as part of the plan. A large proportion of drives are far too narrow, sometimes unavoidably so, but if the space is there, use it. While *you* may get used to the problem, your guests will not be amused by Houdini-style exits via quarter-open doors, or a mere six inches of concrete between the car and a vicious line of rose bushes. It is not necessary to construct a section of motorway, just bear in mind that where cars are boarded and evacuated you should allow the width of the vehicle plus a good three feet on either side.

POOLS

While ornamental pools undoubtedly require more maintenance than the equivalent space filled with shrubs, they are a nice feature and are not really gardening anyway. The siting of pools is important. They should not be under trees that lose their leaves, for obvious reasons, nor should they be in areas exposed to strong sunlight all day because this will encourage unwanted algae growth that turns the contents of the pool green. They need some shade.

You can plan your pool in the ground or above the ground. Few are more than eighteen inches deep and they can be any shape you want. But the type of pool construction you use may depend on how rigid your requirements are. More about this later. Just stick one in on the plan and worry about how to make it when the time comes.

SLOPING GROUND

Ground with a substantial slope naturally lends itself to either a series of steps, or to terracing, achieved by a series of retaining walls or features built from natural stone. Rock gardens are most effective set into sloping land and need not take much looking after. Check the funds though, because decent stone is expensive and a few tons won't go very far.

It is possible to create limited slopes on level ground, but only a compulsive digger would consider excavating one end of the garden to make a hill at the other end. *If* you

have a vast quantity of rubble, *if* you are excavating for a patio, drive, or garage base, *if* you are prepared to buy in a load of topsoil – then make a slope by all means. But it's only really worth it to solve a problem; don't go and create one.

VEGETABLE BITS

Common sense governs most basics of plotting a garden, and it's obviously sensible to site the less attractive vegetable patch – if you decide to have one – away from the house. This portion of the garden can be screened off by a row of taller shrubs, or you could be really daring and use fruit trees as a divider. Cordon type trees, i.e. ones that are kept 'flat' in a vertical plane, would be ideal ... but we're starting to get enthusiastic now.

While you don't particularly design areas for bonfires and rubbish heaps, it is nevertheless as well at least to consider which part of the garden will be so graced. There might just be an awkward corner that could be filled by a simmering compost heap, with any luck luring flies away from where you are.

A greenhouse might appeal, if for no other reason than to store overflow items from the house, garage, shed etc. This should be close to the productive section of the garden, unless you fancy a lean-to version against one side of the house. But if you get a greenhouse you'll certainly be expected to grow something in it – like more tomatoes than you can eat.

SCREENS

'Screens' covers everything from walls to fences, hedges, rows of trees, shrubs, or whatever. We don't count parked caravans, lines of washing or smoke.

In labour-saving terms, walls take first prize, and low, ornamental ones are not startlingly expensive. Where you will get caught is on a brick or stone boundary wall, particularly if you don't feel confident enough to raise one up to six feet high yourself and have to call in a builder. So plan the inclusion of walls with care and remember that, logically, they should be constructed first. Walls and fences don't take up a lot of room, but if it's a hedge screen you go for, allow for the extra width and be prepared to wait for the thing to grow. Hedges, it is said, are more effective screens than solid objects because they filter wind rather than deflect it over the top and down again. I'm sure that's true, but frankly I've never been able to detect any major difference.

Screen blocks make attractive dividers and have the advantage, or disadvantage, that you can see through them at a ninety-degree angle, but they form a solid surface from around forty-five degrees. They can be used to good effect in conjunction with brickwork.

* * *

Having got some idea of how you intend to transform the outer regions, loosely known as your garden, it's a good idea to draw up the master plan to scale on graph paper. Apart from getting everything in proportion, this is also a constant reference for estimating materials and saves going outside to measure something every five minutes.

Don't be afraid of creating shapes. Curves can quite easily be plotted out by eye on site, and there are simple ways of describing circles, ovals, squares and so on. The only point to bear in mind is that it will be more difficult to put curves in paving and walls, so it might be best to take the easy way and keep those straight while doing the fiddly bits with lawns and borders.

GEOMETRY

The level of geometry required to meet our basic needs has been known for thousands of years, so if they could do it with Stonehenge it's a matter of personal pride that we ought to be able to master the problem ourselves.

Circles are the ultimate in simplicity. Knock a peg into the ground at the centre of the proposed ring and attach a line to it by means of a loop. Tie a marker (pointed stick) to the other end at the radius you need and mark out the edge, keeping the line taut. Don't tie the line to the centre peg or it will shorten as you go round. And we all know what happens to people who go round in ever decreasing circles ...

Squares are more devious, but are still within our power aided by the magic 3, 4, 5 triangle. This is a foolproof way of making right angles. The machinations can appear quite incomprehensible to any untutored onlookers, so make sure you have an audience when doing this one.

The principle is that if the base of your triangle measures say three feet, the side measures four feet and the sloping face five feet, then the angle where the three-foot and four-foot lines meet must be ninety degrees. Try it on a piece of paper in inches to get the idea. The same applies to any multiples of 3, 4, 5 such as 6, 8, 10 or 12, 16, 20, so we can deal with any size square we are likely to encounter in the garden. As a rule, the side must always be longer than the intended square for greater accuracy.

Armed with this background, we make a loop of a section of line that is exactly twelve feet long (three feet plus four feet plus five feet, or multiples as needed) and mark the divisions. For simplicity let's say we want to mark out a three-foot square. The base line will have been established, so pegs go in at either end and the loop placed over them with the three foot division matching up to the pegs. With another peg we then merely have to position it so that the line is taut against the four-foot marker. There is your right angle. The next step is to measure three feet along the side, put in a peg and move the triangle around to do the same thing along the top. Then joining up the last and first pegs will complete the square. That may sound complicated, but study the diagram and you'll get the idea in no time at all.

Ovals are quite popular and can easily be mapped out with a couple of pegs and a length of line. Knock two into the ground at each end and inside the proposed length of the oval. How far inside they are placed will affect the oval's width; the further inside they are, the wider it will be. Make a loop of the line which, when placed over the pegs and pulled outwards, will coincide with the width available. Then, holding a marker peg inside the loop and keeping it taut, mark out the shape by moving round the central pegs. Good fun, isn't it?

By now, you're probably enjoying things so

HOW TO CREATE THE CIRCLE

Bang peg in at centre of proposed circle.

Loop – do not tie – rope over said peg.

Measure off radius on rope and tie marker peg at appropriate distance.

Inscribe circle on verdure.

Nobody likes a smart-arse

WRONG

RIGHT

THE RIGHT ANGLE

5 feet

4 feet

Your Right Angle →

3 feet

The old 3·4·5 Triangle Method guarantees perfect Right Angles – this way lies happiness in your squares and rectangles.

Final check on your right angles – Measure from corner to corner and if measurements are equal – you are in business.

Your marker (KEEP TAUT)

Bang 2 pegs in inside oval-to-be.

Distance between pegs will determine width of Oval.

Place loop over pegs allowing sufficient play so that your marker when inserted creates poetic oval.

VAUXHALL END

THE OVAL

much you fancy sticking a *triangle* in somewhere just for the sake of it. If so, why not hazard an equilateral one – that's the sort where all three sides are equal, as if you didn't know. Mark out one side to the required length with two pegs, attach a line to one of them and tie a marker peg to the other end at a distance equal to the base line. Holding the line taut, inscribe a generous arc somewhere above the centre of the base line. Move over to the other peg and do the same. Where the two arcs cross, slot in another peg and there's your actual equilateral triangle.

Performing these feats will, with any luck, be a dazzling display of intellect, the secrets to be passed on only in return for some favour. Those original Stonehenge surveyors I mentioned earlier were no doubt held in great awe by the minions, and still are today come to that. While our twentieth century geometric garden might not enjoy the same status for quite as long, it can hardly fail to produce a modest period of speculation, and maybe even adulation.

2. Escape Routes

The Cover-Up

It follows that ground covered with a degree of permanence will be easier to maintain than ground which has to be worked by digging, planting, weeding, lifting, storing, re-planting, mulching, hoeing, feeding, tying up, cutting down ... sorry about that. Got quite carried away for a moment.

The normal reaction, if it is suggested that as much surface area as possible should be put under restraint, is that you propose a large and uninteresting expanse, more akin to a car park than a garden. Such a vision is ludicrously unjustified as we shall demonstrate. No unattainable skill is involved in producing an attractive sealed unit, and the aftercare is vastly reduced. It is not practical to cut out work altogether – after all, everyone should have a bath at least once a year, whether they need one or not.

THE CASE FOR GRASS
The most common form of mass ground cover is the lawn. Lawns have the advantage of being relatively cheap to produce, can be any shape under the sun, are largely self-perpetuating, are green most of the time, can

be used for games, and can be sat on. The disadvantages are that they need cutting frequently, cannot be used when wet, and often become besieged by undesirables such as moss and daisies which can be extremely difficult to get rid of.

But, provided that we are not expecting to produce a bowling green surface, the case for lawns as labour savers has become increasingly strong. The main reason for this has been the appearance of the cheap, electric mower, bringing the luxury of powered cutting to millions more people. It isn't that long ago that the motor mower had a very upmarket place in the gardening world, and could never be justified for small areas of grass. Now, cutting the average lawn is no more strenuous than vacuum cleaning a carpet. More important, it can even be done by other members of the family who had previously escaped the chore by reason of insufficient physical strength. The novelty value alone can produce a steady stream of volunteers, at least for a while.

Lawns are notorious for their prodigious rate of growth, particularly during warm, wet summers when it seems that they are bent on some feat of super-regeneration specifically to cancel out every assault you might make. At one stage my household included a pair of guinea pigs, which shared the same degree of fertility, so it seemed sensible to match the two forces. Each day the herd was turned loose on the lawn, contained within a three-foot square cage. By moving the cage up and down the lawn we had what, in effect, was a living mower, as the ravenous beasts cropped the grass. It was certainly possible to cover the whole area within a week, at which point you started the cycle all over again. Droppings had to be swept up, but that was no great problem. Population control was the most significant drawback, the mini-mowers being capable of multiplying to attain such numbers that they might comfortably have taken on an entire field. Sadly the overall scheme had to be judged only a partial success, but you might like to give it a try. Watching the little devils thrashing up and down, devouring grass as fast as they could, was moderately entertaining – and must have given the lawn something to think about.

It is possible to treat grass with a chemical that retards its growth – this is available as Superlec, marketed by Synchemicals. It is not widely used, being fairly expensive. And it would be just our luck to retard the lawn just before an unexpected drought, and then the whole thing would probably die off – a desperation measure only, I think.

Naturally slow growing grass is also on the market, but its obvious asset is also its biggest disadvantage. Lawns from such seed take longer to establish and longer to recover from any damage. But if your lawn isn't going to suffer a lot of wear then it could be worth inquiring about at your local garden centre. On the whole, a standard grass seed mixture or reasonable quality turf are your best bets, given ease of cutting.

PAVING THE WAY

The next most common cover-up, in terms of the area shielded, is paving. Patios, paths, drives and even entire gardens are executed by this means, providing a surface of great durability requiring only sweeping.

It is extremely simple to produce attractive paved areas today. Slabs produce the most formal effect but are obtainable in many shapes, sizes and colours. Many eye-catching patterns can be created by using just three basic sizes. It is wise to avoid large areas such as patios made up of uniform slabs, because it's boring.

Paving is one of the most satisfying construction jobs, each piece solving a digging or weeding job forever and creating a nice clean part to walk on. It's almost like building a bridge to reach hitherto untraversed regions; you can develop a real pioneer spirit as you open up the really grotty parts of your garden. The transformation afterwards can be compared with laying a carpet on bare floorboards.

Some continuity, or repetition of a theme, is desirable when paving, rather than a random filling in of holes. This also applies to colours, when going for a range of greys, pinks, yellows, charcoal etc. This approach means you don't really want a random selection of slabs or stones to fill a specified area. It is best to make a reconnaissance trip to your local supplier to get details of the range of sizes/colours/prices available, and then devise your pattern on paper. Generally you only need to make up the section that is going to be repeated, and then see how many of those same sections will be needed to cover the area concerned. By simply counting the number of any particular sized (or coloured) slab to be used, you can then go along with an accurate order. Thus you will avoid special trips to change slabs, buy more, or ending up with too many.

For more tricky sections, particularly where paving is on two or more levels, an idiot-proof method I've used myself is to cut pieces of card to the sizes of slab you'll be using (scaled down of course) and then use them like a jigsaw puzzle to achieve a good fit with a consistent pattern. The size of slabs and how they go together will influence the width of some sections, since it is infinitely preferable to work with complete units all the time than to have to start cutting odd pieces. It is not always possible to avoid a certain amount of cutting, but this should be kept to a minimum.

Having completed your jigsaw, mark the colours on each piece so that it can then be dismantled, sorted into sizes and colours and counted. *Don't* make the nightmare mistake of shuffling the pieces up before you've committed the loose plan to paper ... having spent some hours getting your plan exactly right, there can be nothing more mentally stunning than to be happily counting the pieces when you suddenly realise there isn't a plan to work from any more. It's enough, as they say, to make a saint kick a hole in a stained glass window.

Your slabs will in all probability be delivered. Try to get them off-loaded close to where you'll be using them. Reconstituted stone is particularly dense and heavy, not recommended for moving any distance by hand. Slabs are specially designed for trapping fingers when stacking, slipping out of fingers and falling on feet, causing back and other more grievous injuries when lifting. Treat them with respect and they're the reluctant gardener's best friends.

Dropping every other slab could leave you with a fabulous range of random shapes, the basis of crazy paving. But natural stone is best for this – though it is often possible to buy quantities of broken slabs from local councils or similar sources. No pre-determined plan is required for crazy paving; you simply place the bits together as you go along. It makes a really nice surface, far less formal than straight edged slabs, especially with the irregular face texture which you get with natural material, such as York stone. The crazy paving method is more widely used for paths than patios, because it will work round corners easily and is not going to have someone trying to make a table or chair stand level on it. Broken reconstituted stone is the exception, because it usually has a flat face.

BRICKS, COBBLES AND WOOD
Bricks can also be used for surfacing, mostly laid side on but not so that they resemble a horizontal wall. Repetitive patterns can be devised, one of the most popular being the familiar herringbone seen in connection with wood-block floors. Old or new bricks are suitable, preferably with a faced edge. Your area to be covered will take longer to complete because of the small units, of course, and if the bricks are too old they will quickly crumble under heavy traffic. When you think about it, the last thing a brick expects is to be walked on. But they will tolerate the abuse for a fair while and brick paths are commonly described as giving a 'rustic' effect. Arrrh.

You can always break up a more conventionally paved area with aesthetically placed units of bricks. This also applies to cobbles, except that in their case a practical reason for their use can be put forward: cobbles – egg-sized rounded stones set in cement – are very uncomfortable to walk on. So, if there's part of the patio you want pedestrians to avoid, such as round an isolated and low-lying plant that is just asking to be trodden on, a cobble barrier will reduce the probability. It won't have the slightest effect on cats and dogs, who seem immune even to the roughest surfaces, and in my experience go out of their way to try them out. But since we are going for plants with a strong instinct for survival, they will fully expect to be jumped on by a fairy elephant of some species now and again.

Now, if you once had a fairly large tree in the garden that had to be felled, there's a way of getting rid of some of it. Slices of tree, treated with preservative, make wonderful wooden paving. The rings need to be packed tight together to form an almost continuous surface, so if you have a lot of large pieces, you'll need a lot of smaller ones as well to fill in. And the harder the wood, the longer it will last. If the tree is a very old one, rotten in the centre, forget it. But if you fancy this idea, get hold of a power saw – because hacking through endless pieces of wood up to a foot in diameter really isn't tempting, unless a crash course in bicep building turns you on.

CONCRETE FOR QUICKNESS
Concrete has to be another significant means of mastering large areas of Mother Earth. It is most suitable for drives and paths, and isn't particularly difficult to apply once the preparation work has been done. Concrete isn't the most attractive surface by

any stretch of the imagination, but large areas can be covered in half a day if you buy the stuff ready mixed.

Mixing cement yourself is only really worthwhile for small sections, or when you're building walls, laying paving etc. The speed at which we can work will govern the amount of cement to be mixed in one go, particularly in hot weather when it dries out very quickly. In the true traditions of unarmed do-it-yourself, most of my mixing has been done with an old garden trowel, succeeded by a child's beach spade which was commandeered in a moment of ruthlessness inspired by desperation. Mind you, I was able to return the utensil, stronger than ever with its very own reinforcing layer of cement. This, of course, was my sole object from the beginning – wasn't it?

The bulk delivery of ready mixed concrete, by giant mixer lorry, is an awe-inspiring sight. First, there is an element of panic as the machine churns out a great heap of concrete which starts to spread all over the place. This is followed by demented shovelling and barrowing, to get the unwieldy mass in position and flattened out while it is still workable. Once it was my great misfortune to receive an eagerly awaited prototype load one hour earlier than anticipated. While in a state of utter confusion, I completely forgot that my car was still in the garage, while the heap spread out all over the drive. Such an elementary bungle is difficult to credit and even more difficult to get out of, gracefully or otherwise. Try not to make the same mistake.

Though we shall deal with the mechanics later, it is worth mentioning now that concrete paths can have patterns drawn on them to give a fake crazy paving effect. This can be done with a stick, and you can't get much more basic than that.

TARMAC AND GRAVEL
Nowhere near so widely used domestically, but still an alternative for drives, is tarmac. Cold tarmac or asphalt mixes can be bought in bags and are certainly easier to apply than hot preparations. But, like everything, if it's easier it costs a little more. The top coat is

spread over a coarser foundation mixture, which must be absolutely level. When spread out, the tarmac is rolled, which involves obtaining something like a vibrating roller from a plant hire company. Such a surface is very durable but can become soft and sticky in very hot weather, as do some of our roads. Its main advantage over concrete is that very large areas can be covered in one go, whereas concrete would have to be laid in sections. You could also roll in coloured granite chippings to give your drive a special quality.

As a loose covering, gravel is still common enough and infinitely cheaper than solid forms. It's an economic way of covering long drives, provides a pleasant texture and answers back with crunchy sounds. But it spreads all over the place. And have you ever tried clearing snow from gravel? Nowadays, common gravel is supplemented by several variations, including man-made stones of identical shape but various colours. Also you might be able to get hold of flat shale discs, which at least don't roll about.

SPREADING AND CREEPING
So far we've only considered lawns as a means of live ground cover, but there are many more possibilities for those awkward places where it would be difficult to mow or just for the sake of fixing for good a portion of delinquent ground. Perhaps the most intriguing option is camomile, which grows about three inches tall, has a perfume, can be different colours, and can even be mown! Complete camomile lawns can still be found, but these are expensive to produce and need a sunny, moist position. Nevertheless, camomile will fill a fair area pretty swiftly and needs no fussy maintenance. It can even be used for making tea, if you have the recipe.

Other alternatives for ground cover include:

Periwinkle (Vinca) is excellent, growing very quickly and doing well in sunny or shaded positions. It is evergreen and spreads by means of the tips rooting. This also makes it very easy to propagate because you can detach newly formed plantlets to start a bed somewhere else. It carries blue-purple flowers over a long period and can be mutilated at intervals without any ill effect.

St John's Wort (Hypericum) spreads rapidly, providing lots of colour for most of the summer, and is mostly a yellow shade. It will thrive in any position and may be trimmed with shears to maintain control.

A larger shrub is *Herringbone (Cotoneaster horizontalis)* which is adaptable for wall cover as well as ground. Herringbone is descriptive of the branch pattern. The small green leaves change to scarlet in autumn when scarlet berries also appear. It might be a bit expensive as pure ground cover, but will span five feet and makes an attractive feature.

Ivy (Hedera) is more often associated with wall cover and house plants, but it also smothers ground and may need clipping back regularly.

Archangel (Lamium) is rampant and cheap, carrying yellow or pink-purple flowers in early summer. It will operate well in partial shade and in poor soils.

Creeping Willow (Salix repens) is ideal on really wet soils and is one of the taller feature subjects.

Heathers (Erica), though a bit expensive, are among the most versatile cover-up aids. Planted in groups they will soon fill quite a large area and there are varieties to flower in spring, summer, autumn and winter. Once established they can be clipped back immediately after flowering to maintain a compact form. Most heathers prefer an acid soil but the *Winter Heath (Carnea)* grows well on lime and there are many types from which to choose.

Pachysandra, for which there is no generally known common name, is a small spreading plant, evergreen, and can reach up to twelve inches in height. It grows very well in shade, particularly in dry soil beneath trees. The green-white flowers are insignificant, but shiny green foliage makes it popular.

Two versions of *Partridge Berry* are worth consideration – those known as *Gaultheria procumbens* and *Shallon. Procumbens* is a dwarf, creeping shrub about six inches tall. The white and pink flowers of autumn are followed by crimson-pink berries. It grows quickly in shade. *Shallon* is a larger species, flowering in early summer and particularly prolific in dry, shady situations.

If you like mint either for cooking or in sauces, I dare you to plant a sprig. It's more like a weed than a weed, and can cover vast areas at an epidemic rate. The more bits you pull off the more it will grow. If only the majority of plants shared its enthusiasm ...

A Tale of Horticultural Espionage

Cubby Broccoli's

GREENFINGER

starring

SEAN CONIFER
ROGER MOWER

LORNE GREEN - SOPHIA LUPIN
GINA LOBELIA - SIDNEY GREENHOUSE

2. Escape Routes Survivors

Survival is such a basic instinct that you might wonder why it is that plants in the hands of non-skilled or semi-skilled gardeners suffer such a high fatality rate. In the natural state plants survive because they become adapted to suit their environment; a radical change in environment will obviously have a disastrous effect on those plants, while others, which had previously struggled for existence, might suddenly find that all is now to their advantage. It's like going from supplementary benefit to a half-million pools success, or the other way round.

This is of course a great over-simplification of vegetable evolution, and there are many other factors that influence a plant's chances in the horticultural rat race. But it helps to answer the query as to why some plants survive and some don't.

The main problem is that we constantly attempt to grow things in conditions for which they are totally unsuited. If we can resist that temptation, choosing plants that have particularly high tolerance to all kinds of conditions, then it logically follows that the prospects of survival are vastly improved. The super-plant will need to cope with rapid weather variations, lack of water, too much water, and, in all probability, abuse of a very general nature. But there are no guarantees; casualties are inevitable even in the most fanatically maintained garden. Even weeds have been known to perish of their own accord. There must have been at least ten this century.

UNRAVELLING NAMES

Most people shy away from the proper names of plants, understandably so because the pronunciation possibilities are legion and it's much easier to remember a Flaming Poppy than *Meconopsis heterophylla*. However, the full botanical titles not only group plants into families but often give a very accurate description of appearance or habit. The two or three word tongue-twisters are divided into a family name, in effect the surname, and a descriptive or adjective which is the christian name. Put together, these names identify a quarter of a million or so known species, using mainly Latin.

While common names are in general used throughout this book, it is nevertheless worth having a brief look at some of the proper ones. They can help us pick out plants to suit our needs, and detect others to be avoided.

If we take generic surnames first, then *anastatica* would appear helpful, being derived from the Greek *anastasis*, which means resurrection. This is interpreted as being resistant to drought. The same ability to survive in dry conditions is given to the group *arabis*, meaning from Arabia.

Nothing would seem to rival *sempervivum* (Houseleek) which gets its name from the Latin *sempervivere*, to be immortal. But we can also be encouraged by *anemone*, from *anemos* meaning wind, indicating a home in exposed places.

Rapid growth is expressed in several families, including *anethum* (*ano* – upwards, *theo* – I run), *itea* meaning willow and suggesting quick progress in damp conditions, and *raphanus*, which is radish, and contrived from *ra* (quickly) and *phainomai* (appear). (Nothing about repetition here though.)

Anthemis (*anthemon* – a flower) is said to identify the family as being profuse at flowering, while *diosma* (*dios* – divine, *osme* – scent) obviously refers to a pleasant smell.

It's quite a good game when you get into it, isn't it?

Heliophila (*helios* – sun, *phile* – love) speaks for itself in enjoying a sunny spot, whereas the opposite is stated by *episcia* (*epischia* – shade).

You might be attracted by the quite remarkable qualities of *herniaria*, coarsely known as Rupturewort. The name is derived from hernia, which allegedly can be cured by the plant. Think twice before taking home *anacampseros* (*anakampto* – to cause to return) which is claimed to restore passion. Equally hazardous potentially is the family *oenothera* (*oinos* – wine, *thera* – imbibing), one relative thought to promote wine drinking. But *anagallis* seems pleasant enough, taken from *anagalao* – to laugh.

It seems sensible to avoid *achimenes*, which translated means to suffer from cold, and therefore being too tender for our needs. And the *lupinus* household, christened after wolf, is branded as a destroyer. Should the need arise, one way of attracting baboons into the garden (well, it makes a change from birds) is to plant *babiana*, which got its name because baboons are extremely partial to the bulbs.

Now on to words which give the specific nature of individuals. Many are easily interpreted, illustrating the origin of portions of our own language.

Instantly appealing are:
amabilis – lovely;
diutinus – long-lasting or spreading;
divergens – spreading;
festivus – pleasant;
fragrans – fragrant;
mirabilis – amazing;
sempervivus – everlasting;
trimus – three-year life;
validus – strong;
vivus – lively.

Make a mental note, too, of:
ascendens – ascending;
heli – sun-loving;
argillaceus – clay-loving;
coccifera, baccatus or *baccifera* –
　having berries;
dejectus or *depressus* – low-lying;
dependens – hanging down;
decumanus – immense;
erectus – upright;
gypsophilus – chalk-loving;
horizontalis – horizontal growing;
luxurians – excessive growth;
muralis – wall covering;
nanus – dwarf;
patens – spreading.

Beware of:
amarus – disagreeable;
caducus – frail;
corcopherus – has bugs;
debilis – feeble;
felosmus – smells terrible;
horridus – looks horrible;
impatiens – no endurance;
incomptus – rude;
miser – pitiable;
pruriens – has a sting or causes
　itching;
verenatus or *zooctonus* – poisonous.

And particularly strange seem:
anthelminticus – kills worms;
antidysenticus – anti-dysentery;
catharticus – purgative;
hircinus – smelling like a goat;
and *porcinus* – to do with pigs.

So much for the background to plant selection and what some of the funny words mean. We now return to simplicity and gain new hope from the elite among survivors.

BULBS

For simplicity, try these: Daffodils, Crocuses, Grape Hyacinths, Snowdrops, Golden Garlic (*A l i u m   m o l y*) and Cyclamen (*neapolitanium*). All come up year after year and multiply. They can also be planted in grass, providing an excuse for not cutting it until the foliage has died down.

HARDY ANNUALS

There's a lot to be said for plants grown from seed spread around in the garden. Most need no attention except watering in the early stages. However, once their survival period is over, they will die and not flower again. Particularly recommended are:

Marigold (*Calendula*) which will seed to give more next year without extra work;

Convolvulus and Cornflower which will grow almost anywhere;

Nasturtium, impossible to fail with even in poor soil;

Godetia, best in sunny positions;

Poppy, a super-reliable plant giving lots of colour;

Sweet Peas, thrive in most soils and dwarf types need no support;

Sweet Sultan, easy to grow and good for cutting;

Larkspur;

and the giant Sunflower, which will easily reach eight feet, while specimens over twenty feet are possible.

HERBACEOUS PERENNIALS

Those recommended here are cheap and colourful and most spread rapidly. The only maintenance required is watering and an autumn trim to keep them tidy, and their great advantage is that they come up year after year.

Monkshood (*Aconitum*), grows anywhere and has strong, wiry stems;

Columbine (*Aquilegia*), is short-lived, but seeds all over the place for continuity;

Elephants' Ears (*Bergeria*), carries large leaves and suppresses weeds;

Michaelmas Daisy (*Aster*), comes in a wide range of colours and the clumps expand quickly;

Campanula, a tough and vigorous plant that is low-lying and simple to grow;

Coreopsis, another tough customer that is very good on clay;

Foxglove (*Digitalis*), often appears uninvited but carries large purple or blue flowers on spikes;

Echinops spreads rapidly;

Geranium, creeping roots make it a fast spreader;

Iris, bearded varieties very easy to grow in hot, sunny spots;

Mimulus, grows quickly in wet or dry conditions;

Forget-me-not (*Myosotis*), just throw down a handful of seeds and they'll grow;

Cat Mint (*Nepeta*), seeds frantically;

Polygonum, grows and spreads very fast;

Saxifrage and Sedium, ideal for rock gardens ˌˑd in stone walls;

Veronica, will ramble all over borders.

SHRUBS

The selection below are all permanent, and once planted need very little attention.

Snowy Mespilus (*Amelarchier*), grows in any old soil;

Spotted Laurel (*Aucuba*), grows anywhere and is immune to exhaust fumes and drips from trees, if that's any use to you;

Barberries (*Berberis*), tough and spiky, needs no attention and used as a hedge will keep out dogs, cats and people;

Butterfly Plant (*Buddleia*), a large bush that will fill a lot of space. Best if pruned every year, but this isn't essential;

Heathers (*Erica*), most need acid soil but spread well;

Japonica (*Chaenomeles*), grows anywhere unattended;

Dogwood (*Cornus*), a big and fast grower – and a variegated version is available. Prune every autumn for good, dark colour;

Cotoneaster, loads of varieties, some tall, some spreading, some evergreen. Grows anywhere with total neglect;

Hawthorn (*Crataegus*), good, cheap hedging that's fast and not fussy;

Broom (*Cytissus*), needs clipping to keep shape but will tolerate bad treatment;

Deutzia, large and showy, bushes best in an exposed spot;

Spindle Bush (*Euonymus*), a native plant that will thrive anywhere;

Forsythia, easily pleased but best pruned after flowering;

Hydrangea, super flowers and needs no pruning or special conditions;

Holly (*Ilex*), slow growing but good in towns;

Kernia, plant it and forget it;

Mahoria, good and effortless evergreen for shade;

Snowball Tree (*Philadelphus*), cheaply bought large bush;

Cinquefoil (*Potentilla*), a small, dome-shaped shrub that grows anywhere and flowers prolifically;

Flowering Currant (*Ribes*), cheap and easy to grow;

Elder (*Sambucus*): Golden Elder is especially good, growing swiftly and unaided;

Bridal Wreath (*Spiraea*), always succeeds;

Snowberry (*Symphoricarpus*), really a weed but who's checking?;

Lilac (*Syringa*), large, strong bushes;

Viburnam, ultra-simple and flowers in spring and winter;

Weigelia, flourishes regardless but needs post-flowering pruning to keep tidy.

CLIMBERS

Things to grow against walls, fences, buildings, screens and so on without fiddling are:

Russian Vine (*Polygonum*), extremely fast anywhere;

Honeysuckle (*Lonicera*), vigorous and easy, also has a nice smell;

Virginia Creeper (*Parthenocissus*), self-clinging plant which need trouble you no more after installation;

Ivy (*Hedera*), many varieties are available, some are self-clinging, and they don't damage walls.

ROSES

Not a lot to say about roses, except that they are easy to grow in most gardens and need pruning once a year. Floribundas are strong and very showy while Hybrid Teas are best for cutting.

CONIFERS

A vast range exists and most are easy though they might need protection from wind and dogs in the early stages. *Cupressocyparis Leylandii* is the fastest growing hedging.

TREES

All gardens benefit from a tree to give height and a bit of shade. These are some of the best at survival:

Flowering Thorn (*Crataegus*), a small, native tree that grows anywhere;

Flowering Cherry (*Prunus*), very showy and easy to grow but prefers a chalky soil;

Flowering Crabs (*Malus*), great number of varieties and you can eat the fruits as jelly or jam;

Laburnum, simple to grow but poisonous seeds may kill the cat;

Maple (*Acer*), relatives of sycamore so very vigorous as foliage trees. Avoid Japanese varieties which are tender.

Apples and pears, supply the best of both worlds with fruit and flowers;

Cherry Plum (*Prunus cerasifera*), another foliage tree but will grow in any location.

2. Escape Routes

Tools

While it is surprising what can be performed with the proverbial knife and fork, there is no doubt that the gardener's life can be made far easier with the correct tool. It would be fairly logical to assume that the range of equipment carried by a non-enthusiast would be less than that of someone who can actually tell one plant from another. Yet it would be equally reasonable to expect the defensive gardener to have a tool shed like an arsenal, featuring all manner of tactical weaponry to maintain a balance of power with the thing outside.

Though they are not true deterrents, in that the grass will continue to grow even in the face of a savage mower, any uprisings can be swiftly put down if the appropriate strike force is to hand. Though garden equipment is given the image of a beautifying resource, it is nonetheless an aid to suppression, and even destruction. Relate the garden image to the cosmetic market: make-up is promoted for its eventual effect, and no one stresses too heavily what it is covering up.

Motives apart, the range of tools we ought ideally to own will vary according to the type of garden we have. Assuming that not every

piece of equipment will be purchased in one extravagant flourish, priorities will also be influenced by the immediacy and volume of certain maintenance.

Hand tools, counting those that you walk behind or push, can be divided into two prime categories: those that work the soil, and those that cut. There are many other functions, but none quite so fundamental nor so important as these two.

SOIL TOOLS

Working soil is the most gruelling aspect, and into this torment fall some of the most familiar tools. Let us start with *the spade*. Just about every established household must possess a spade. This multi-role implement can be used for digging as in cultivation, digging as in holes, clearing snow, chopping worms in half, squashing snails, flattening other things, knocking sticks into the ground, mixing, and even modest shovelling. The shovel itself is a quite separate utensil, having raised sides in order to contain whatever is being shovelled. A flat-bladed spade can never fully compete in this area, but is definitely first choice if it has to be one or the other.

The inevitable companion to the spade is *the fork*. Though identical with spades in superstructure, forks, with their four or five prongs, have another set of speciality functions. Digging for cultivation is the main one, followed by moving garden rubbish, poking bonfires, stabbing lawns (for soil aeration, not malice) and leaning on. Forks will not in general dig holes, require above average skill to impale worms and snails, but will jam stones between the prongs and go right through potatoes, even if there's only one on the root.

One other major option for digging remains, and that is *the mechanical rotovator*. You would need to be embattled with a fairly large plot of productive land to justify the ownership of one, but for those needing to get untamed land into shape, hiring or borrowing is a good thought. Rotovators consist, in essence, of around eight tilling blades driven by a small engine. They come in many shapes and sizes, but all churn up the ground in a fraction of the time it would take to dig by hand.

However, although actual digging time is greatly reduced, roughly about the same amount of energy is concentrated into it. Left to its own devices, the small rotovator will either dig itself into a hole, or race across the surface to be cultivated. To make the recalcitrant implement work, the novice operator will either be pushing it forward or holding it back, while sinking into the freshly churned soil behind. This can be exhausting work for the unfit, particularly on hard ground when pulling and pushing is accentuated and seldom predictable.

It was my great privilege as an impressionable youth to attend the first trials of a home-made rotovator. This was a leviathan among its fellows, driven by nothing less than a four-cylinder car engine and sitting on four enormous, pronged wheels. Though passing years can exaggerate the event, I swear that as drive was engaged, the monster accelerated to about fifteen mph, dragging its helpless inventor behind. Not a piece of earth was disturbed – just four rows of holes traced the monster's unhindered progress to the grasp of a wire fence. To the best of my knowledge no further trials were staged – quite understandable under the circumstances – but the world may have lost its chance of the first supersonic pea driller.

The chances of anything like this happening to you are remote. Overall, I would say the rotovator is a formidable aid in getting to grips with the defiant garden and thereafter for cultivating any sizeable vegetable patch.

Returning to non-mechanical devices, *the rake* is a fairly standard piece of hardware. It is, would you believe, used for raking – soil level, or things up. The back of the rake is also traditionally adopted for firming soil before and after planting, and if you plan to do any concreting the tool is necessary for spreading. (Makes a mess of it too – the rake, that is.) A medium weapon, the rake is light enough to be brandished at any invading animals likely to be intimidated by a token gesture.

If a fork complements the spade, then the rake is accompanied by *the hoe*. Hoes are for cultivation between plants, either in rows or randomly spaced. There are push types and pull types, but both break up the soil's surface and chop down weeds. They also slice up the bulbs you forgot were there. A secondary role for them is making seed channels, by drawing one corner through the soil, guided by a length of twine. Don't cause embarrassment by asking for a 'heave hoe'.

Coming down the scale, we arrive at those miniature inseparables – *the fork and trowel*. These are the gardener's fine tuners, the fork being used for more fiddly forking and the trowel for making holes to put plants in or, indeed, both can be used for digging plants up. They are a kind of side arm, a far more personal tool than most of the others and in many cases warranting a 'his' and 'hers' arrangement.

There isn't very much more you can buy for strict cultivation. Most of the range of available tools is made up thereafter of variations on themes – sizes, types of handles, manufacturing materials, derivatives for more specialised work, and quality. It is glib advice to say 'buy the best you can afford', but in general better ones will last longer, might

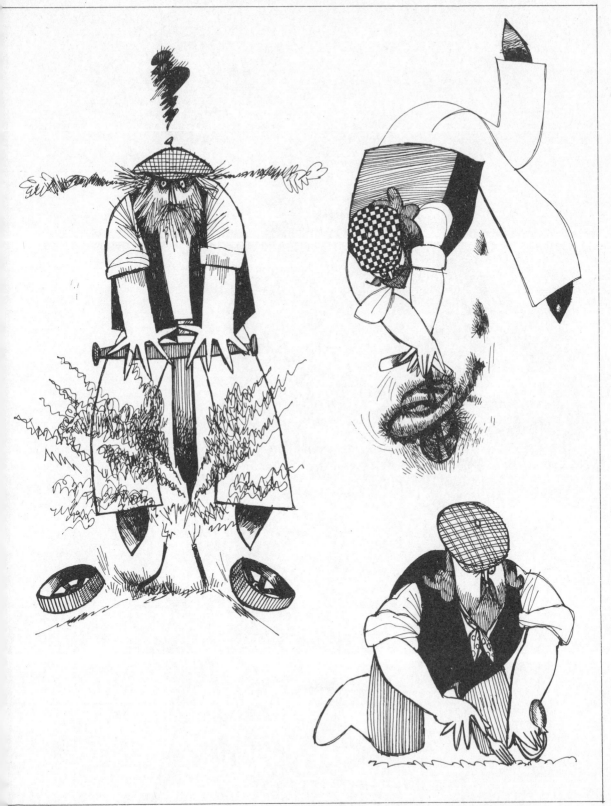

make you look after them, and if you don't then they've still got more chance than a cheap and nasty version.

CUTTING TOOLS

What about cutting tools? First among these comes *the lawnmower*, once a word to chill a man's heart and bring on all manner of muscular afflictions. Anyone who has experienced a few summers campaigning with a badly maintained, hand-propelled mower over an equally pathetically maintained lawn will nod sagely in sympathy. 'Hand-propelled' no more describes the mode of operation than it would satisfactorily define rowing a Byzantine galley from the point of view of a slave oarsman.

Mowing by such means requires considerable exertion, the machine operating in a series of short bursts, frequently locking solid and dragging up great patches of grass. The perfect mower on a perfect lawn would be another matter. But we're not in that league, are we?

As mentioned earlier, twentieth century technology, inspired by the recognition of man's basic laziness, has saved us with the inexpensive, electric mower which began life as little more than an electric drill on wheels. Two main species are featured – the cylinder mower and the rotary mower. Each have their advantages and disadvantages.

Cylinder models have conventional blade arrangements, cutting grass against a horizontal bar. The better ones have a cylinder wheel at the back, like a small roller, which might be driven as well as the blades to save pushing. This variety of mower will usually cut grass shorter and the roller helps iron out small, soft undulations. It will not have any beneficial effect on large depressions, because if it pushes down the peaks it will also push down the hollows. The same can be said for any roller used indiscriminately.

Rotary mowers are flatter, the grass being scythed down by twin horizontally whirling blades within a protected compartment. They are extremely simple and are generally pushed around the lawn as you would vacuum clean a carpet. Rotary models will not crop grass as closely as cylinder mowers,

but they will deal with longer grass and are certainly easier to use when the lawn is wet. All the cheaper forms come with a good length of cable which you must avoid chopping up along with the grass. Either form is best with a grass-collecting box attached, otherwise you'll have cuttings all over the place.

If the green area is a) considerable and b) distant from the nearest power point, then you might consider either a battery or petrol-engined machine. Both are self-propelled, battery mowers giving around two hours' use before needing to re-charge, while motor models will go all day as long as you keep putting fuel in. Both will cost more than the plug-in type, and some petrol burners are not unlike a combine harvester in noise output.

For the really decadent, there are powered tools exclusively made to cut the parts that others cannot reach. One such aid resembles a sparkler on the end of a thick stick, flailing round to apprehend the grass close to trees and in awkward corners. This is a job that could be performed by another cutting tool, *the shears*.

Shears are the things you have to resort to when the lawn is allowed to grow so long that a normal mower will not make any impression. This is a nasty hands and knees job, during which fervent vows are taken not to allow the same thing to happen again. The second time it is viewed as a penance for repeating the mistake and subsequent occasions are grimly endured with a determination to get rid of the lawn as soon as possible. Such outsize scissors should be kept in their place (ideally in the wrapping paper) appearing only for the finishing touches to a lawn edge, though you can get special long-handled ones for that which permit the dignity of standing.

Shears do have another function, which is cutting hedges and routing unruly shrubs. But here again, there is a power alternative, well worth the investment if hedges are your particular curse. Electric hedge trimmers can be bought in remote or plug-in forms, with which you can attack quite substantial woody growth. Because they make the task so easy, there is a tendency to over-kill ... and it's a fair bet that behind every slaughtered hedge lurks a new trimmer owner. Just one obstacle remains: a fortune awaits the manufacturer of a trimmer that picks up all the bits as well.

Down the scale again we come to *secateurs*, a must for anyone with roses or who just likes chopping pieces off here and there. Secateurs are for pruning, a great gardening art which can be much enjoyed by the casual gardener because it is one of the most leisurely tasks. You may also use them for cutting string, drawing it across the one sharp blade, but try to resist pulling out nails with your secateurs, or for that matter applying them to imposing branches. These instruments are normally designed to deal with anything up to half-an-inch in diameter; attempted amputations beyond that size can cause grievous damage to their joints, and you should stir yourself to fetch a saw instead.

That should complete your priority range of cutting tools. Others can be added as you go along, but most from now on will have a precise purpose. For example, a lawn edger, used periodically for sharpening up the sides of lawns by slicing a small strip off, is of no use for anything else that I can think of. The blade is roughly half-moon shaped and ideal for the job: the same effect can be achieved with a spade, with only slightly more difficulty.

ANCILLARY TOOLS
Among the ancillary tools that do not fall into one of the prime categories, a *wheelbarrow* would certainly be helpful in the early stages of creating a garden. It is at this point that the major moving about has to be done and transporting anything, whether it is soil, sand, stone, rubbish, or paving, is that much simpler with a wheel underneath. By the very nature of the exercise, future use will be somewhat limited so it's a case of deciding if the expense is justified.

The *watering can* and *hose pipe* are tools of a sort, and can play a long-term active part. Besides relaying water from tap to plant, they also come in handy for mixing cement, swilling down permanent surfaces, cleaning cars and even putting out fires, if you're not careful. Everybody likes playing with a hose pipe. It requires no effort other than getting the thing out and putting it back. And an adjustable nozzle to provide various forms of spray can give many hours of entertainment. Few people in my experience can resist squirting anything that moves, if for no other reason than to demonstrate their accuracy.

One final necessity is a *brush*. The beauty of extensive paving and other permanent surfaces is that brushing becomes the major form of maintenance, a most elementary skill you must admit. Always sweep downwind, and choose a brush with good strong bristles. There appear to be options on sweeping, with the utensil held to the front or to the side. Each requires a different grip and in the latter case, the brush is in fact being applied backwards to develop more power at the bristles. This reverse thrust is used to move more stubborn debris, such as leaves which have become stuck.

Mechanical sweepers can be bought but they have to be pushed along and have no integral power. What the concrete gardener awaits is a cheap, outdoor vacuum cleaner, which can't be that difficult to produce and would make someone a modest fortune.

THE ART OF DIGGING
To round off this section, we might take a brief look at digging – which has long baffled the non-gardener with references to 'single' and 'double' digging of vegetable patches. Single digging is what you have most likely seen other people doing, that is working backwards in rows, filling one trench with the excavated soil from the next and so on. Penetration is to the depth of the fork or spade (and that doesn't mean to the top of the handle!). Double digging is for the really keen, recommended every three to five years, and designed to achieve such benefits as improved drainage, deeper placing of soil conditioners (manure, compost etc) and more scope for root penetration. The method takes a little bit of understanding but is basically similar to single digging, though on a much grander scale. The plot is divided in half and a trench one spade deep and about a foot across is excavated at one end of one half. Soil

from this is parked off the plot against the other half. Into the hole then goes a layer of manure/compost, and the bottom is broken up with a fork. A similar sized trench is then dug behind, soil from this being used to fill the first one. This exercise continues until the whole area has been worked and your final hole is topped up by that heap left over from the initial excavation. Perhaps twice a decade isn't bad for a spot of soil super-charging, though the prospect of tuning a large area might de-tune our ambitions.

3. The Concrete Bit

Here we arrive at the real essence of labour-saving gardens, and attractive ones too. There is nothing within the scope of the basic concrete bit of the garden that we cannot hope to perform. Some stages are certainly a little more nerve-wracking than others, but view them as a kind of therapy: while you're totally engrossed in getting something level or upright, all other matters are wiped from the mind. And the inflated sense of achievement from your first humble wall must compare with all but the greatest marvels of construction.

The important thing with concrete is not to be too concerned about how long it takes to complete a particular part of your plan. Progress is bound to be slow when the techniques are unfamiliar. Yet it is surprising how much matters improve after relatively brief experience – each brick or slab laid teaches something which is passed on to the next, and so on. Strive for the best job possible, but don't expect perfection. Even the experts struggle to make that.

Let's start with concrete itself, and how to make paths and drives. The first thing to consider, and what will determine the type of construction, is the weight they will be expected to bear. We don't require accuracy to within a pound or two – it is quite unnecessary to calculate the milkman's gross tonnage fully loaded with two crates, sixteen pints and a bag of loose change.

CONCRETE PATHS AND DRIVES

A path to take exclusively pedestrian traffic will need little hardcore, perhaps none if the ground is really hard and stable, and about four inches of concrete. Drives, on the other hand, will need to support far greater pressure, and so must obviously be stronger. If a car is the heaviest prospective vehicle, then a six-inch hardcore foundation topped by six inches of concrete will produce a sturdy job. But should the drive have to cater for heavy delivery vehicles it will demand a more substantial base of around nine inches, with a concrete topping of six inches as before. Foundation is the real key to strength.

Having decided on the appropriate combination, the next step is excavating to the correct depth. An important point to remember is that where a path or drive will adjoin house walls, it must under no circumstances come above the damp course. Ideally, two courses of bricks should remain showing below the course. Raising a path or drive too high will mean that the damp course is effectively by-passed, and you'll be able to take up fungi-growing as an indoor hobby.

Boards must now be placed to contain the concrete until it has set. This is known as 'shuttering'. The first move is to knock in stout pegs along the line of the path or drive, checking along their tops for level. For this you will need a long spirit level (or a long, straight piece of wood and a short spirit level). If one side of the path or drive is to adjoin a wall, you still need shuttering to form the 'container', but in this case the wood stays in place and pegs are driven *inside* the area and below the final suface level. On free edges, the pegs are *outside* the shuttering. A better job can be made of drives by using concrete edging pieces, set in position to form a neat and permanent surround.

When setting the level of shuttering, bear in mind that it should slope slightly away from the house so that water can drain safely away. If a drive has to slope towards the house, then some form of drainage will have to be provided. This generally means a soakaway, effectively a large hole filled with rubble and topped by a glazed stone gully which can be bought from builder's merchants. (The gully, that is, not the hole...) The soakaway is sited at the lowest possible point, and should be topped by at least six inches of concrete.

Next, lay your hardcore. This provides an ideal opportunity to dispose of any brick rubble, broken concrete and even bits of old iron or wire. All manner of solid refuse can go into the base of your construction, and be hammered down to make it compact. If you don't have any such rubbish then there might be a neighbour just dying to get rid of his. Failing that, you might have to buy some. In theory, the coarse foundation should then be covered by a finer material and compressed by a hired heavy roller; but I didn't do that with mine and it's still in one piece ten years later. (That last stage isn't necessary at all, of course, with paths.)

With the shuttering in place and the base complete, you're all ready for the concrete. This is the tricky bit. For a drive it is simpler to have the stuff delivered ready mixed, as has already been mentioned. But how much do you want? Having attempted twice to calculate loads, the first time I was miles short and the next time there was a great surplus. Finding somewhere to put an unwanted heap of concrete is no joke, and all sorts of spots get the cover-up treatment long before it was intended.

The best bet is to calculate how many square yards you have to fill, how deep the area is, and then give those figures to the ready mix people. They're certain to have a better idea than you – they've had more practice. The mixture is generally six parts of three-quarter-inch all-in ballast to one part of cement, kept wet enough to maximise working time and help get a decent surface.

Concrete for small areas can be mixed by hand, or by hiring a proper mixer for a few days. They aren't too expensive and save a lot of desperate work.

Whatever the source of your concrete, the material must be spread evenly over the area, being raked out level and fractionally higher than the shuttering. In the case of a big drive and a bulk delivery, make sure you have plenty of unsuspecting helpers as it's important to get the stuff in position as quickly as possible. For finishing you need a level board long enough to span the width. This is drawn across the surface, being tapped up and down to bring moisture, known as 'the fat', to the surface. Any hollows should be filled with concrete scooped away from the hilly parts, and then gone over again with the board. This tapping up and down motion produces ridging, which helps to provide a grippy surface. If a smoother finish is required then you'll have to go over the surface afterwards with a wooden float.

Long sections of drive or path should be divided every ten feet or so by a length of soft wood set across the shuttering to the depth of the concrete. These act as expansion joints, taking up pressure and preventing cracking as the concrete expands and contracts under extremes of temperature.

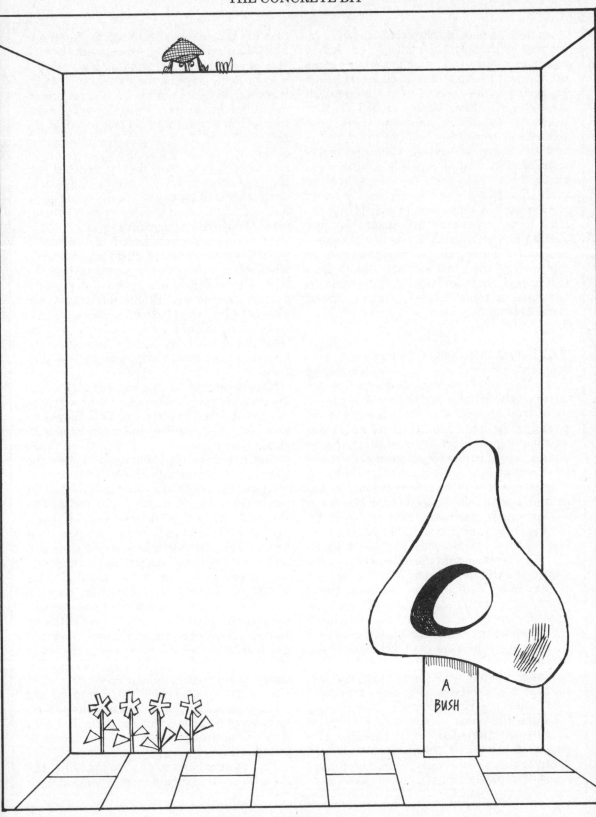

As each section is completed it should be covered with polythene sheets or strong paper, to prevent the concrete hardening too quickly and losing strength. Shuttering can be removed after about a week and full strength will have been reached in four weeks. It would be naive to think that someone or something will not tread on the concrete before it has set. Cats are exceptionally skilled at this, while children can rarely hold back from that experimental prod. To adapt the first moon landing expression – 'A small step for a child, a giant leap from whoever's just spent the day getting it level'. Really it's better to take a resigned attitude, let everybody have a go and inscribe their initials for posterity. You can always cheat and sign a footprint with the name of some living legend. It will be argued about long after you've gone.

PAVED PATHS AND PATIOS

Though very large areas can be covered by concrete in sections, this technique is not particularly suitable for patios. A far more attractive leisure area is achieved with paving slabs and, indeed, paths in certain surroundings look far better in this form. So paving in square and rectangular slabs is our next venture, and again it isn't very difficult.

This type of covering is fairly formal and so demands a reasonably level finish if it is not to look scruffy and blatantly amateurish. By far the easiest method is to lay paving on a bed of sand. To do this you need to be absolutely certain that the area to be covered is firm and will not subside. If such a method is attempted without this condition being met, then in a very short space of time your once flat patio will resemble a budding mountain range with enough tripping features to keep the local casualty department going.

If you're happy with the foundation, then all that needs to be done is any excavation work, allowing for a one-inch layer of sand plus the thickness of the slabs, which is usually one-and-a-half to two inches. The sand bed should be raked smooth, leaped about on to make it compact, and raked level again. Naturally you will have made sure

that the base itself is level before starting to lay slabs directly on top. Adjustments to each slab can be made by tapping down with a wooden tool, perhaps the handle of a heavy hammer, or by ramming loose sand underneath. As you progress, each slab will need to be checked to see that it is level against the rest; with any luck at all, everything will come out right at the end. As you go along, spread sand over the slabs and brush it into the gaps between them. This may have to be done several times to get a really neat finish, but the final result is extremely sturdy considering that no mortar is used.

Use a straight-edged length of wood and a spirit level for constant checking of overall trueness. It is this great concern that gets the adrenalin going and adds to the project's overall excitement. Slight deviations can always be corrected without being obtrusive, and you can afford to scorn such comments as 'That doesn't look level to me' by putting the insignificant defect down to an optical illusion.

Should the site for your patio or path not be too secure, then it is better to play safe and prepare a concrete platform. This should be about four inches thick, and of the same mix as for paths and drives. But without shuttering, how do you go about ensuring that the platform is reasonably level? Such trifling matters will not impede our progress ... for there are ways of making you do it. The simplest method is to use wooden pegs, marked off two and a half inches below their tops. All pegs should be about the same size and are driven into the ground – randomly over a patio area, or in two parallel lines within the final width for a path. Using a length of wood and a spirit level, the pegs can be adjusted until they are all level with one another. The peg tops will then show the finished height of your paving, and the lower marks on them the depth of concrete, which is simply raked in to match up. Paving can start after a couple of days. The protruding peg tops are either driven further into the ground or knocked off as you come to them. But first they are useful for checking the trueness of your paving.

The most common way of applying the slabs is on five points of mortar – one at each corner and one in the middle. The slab is then lowered on to the points and gently tapped down until the correct level is achieved. The accuracy of the first slab is obviously vital, since this will be a guide for all the rest. Constant checks in all directions is the key. An expert would make the whole process look like child's play, but we have to accept our novice status and take things slowly and carefully.

The mix for the mortar is three parts of soft sand to one part of cement; and apart from your straight edged piece of wood and spirit level, you will need a builder's trowel and a club hammer. The hammer is used for tapping into position. Don't bash stubborn slabs with the metal head; always use the handle fairly gently. Slabs might look indestructible, but they crack very easily under over-enthusiastic treatment.

Pointing, that is filling in the gaps between slabs, can be done as you go along or afterwards with the same mortar used for fixing, but a better finish is achieved with a mixture of equal parts sand and cement, used fairly wet so that it more easily fills the crevices. This needs to be done carefully, avoiding getting great dollops of cement over the paving surface, particularly if it is coloured and will mark easily. Pointing might be avoided if slabs are butted together, when sand can be brushed into the small gaps. But some paving is cast with the sides sloping slightly inwards from the bottom – which means that even if they are pressed closely together at the base, there will still be a gap at the top which is better filled.

Theoretically, your new creation, if mortar constructed, should not be used for a couple of weeks. In practice this is seldom the case, but resist the urge to leap all over it for as long as you can.

RAISED SECTIONS

If paving is to be done on two or more levels, then obviously something has to support the higher areas. Walls must be built to form the elevated shapes: single rows of bricks or faced walling stone will normally do, and the inside filled with whatever happens to be handy. This might be a means of getting rid of subsoil excavated from lower parts, rubble etc. If this is tightly packed then you might not need to put in concrete topping. Raised paving should overhang by about half an inch, and it is best to use the larger slabs for edges. Smaller, overhanging pieces can quickly become loose by straightforward leverage when trodden on at the edge. Big ones have sufficient weight and adhesion area to be untroubled.

Creating a raised border within a patio area is just about the same as providing the shell for a raised portion of paving. Instead of laying one or two rows of bricks you will probably go to four, but you are still producing a container which should be given some rubble for drainage and then topped up with soil ready for planting. Many an intended raised bit of paving has ended up as a raised bed on afterthought, and modifications like this are possible during the course of construction. There's nothing wrong with changing your mind provided that it doesn't involve re-doing a lot of work.

CUTTING STONE

Now we must unfortunately look at the grim prospect of having to cut odd pieces of paving in order to secure a fit in awkward places. Some, mainly where there is a fine and close textured grain throughout the slab, cut relatively simply. Others, mostly those with a coarse bulk behind the smooth exterior, can be somewhat trying. It is one thing to understand the principles of cutting, and quite another to accomplish it successfully. Even the most placid character can be aroused during this procedure. There is nothing remotely funny about painstakingly etching the intended point of separation, only to see the slab break in two entirely different pieces. Cutting just seems to be one of those things either you can do or you can't. The single occasion on which I managed to cut a piece of glass cleanly was ruined by the fact that it had been measured two inches short.

Assuming, then, that cutting anything made from concrete in a straight line is next to impossible without a powered masonry saw, it is only worth attempting to cut reconstructed stone with any degree of

This was quite a lively Gardening Centre before the roof caved in

confidence. Tools required are a club hammer and a stone or brick bolster (a broad metal chisel). First, mark where the slab has to be cut with chalk all the way round. Using the bolster and hammer, cut a deep nick in both edges followed by a shallow groove along the chalk lines. Continue tapping along the lines until the slab falls in two (or three, or four ...). It's a great feeling when this process actually works, but even better if you can avoid it all together. If you have a drainpipe to go round, it might be more realistic to use cement for that part, because chipping out an interior curve is infinitely more time consuming and hazardous.

Don't forget to leave out odd slabs here and there if you want to include plants in your patio. This is simple when the paving is being done on a sand base, but slightly more troublesome on a concrete base unless you are able to pinpoint in advance where the gaps will be. Even so, bits of the base can be chiselled out later when you come to plant-hole-location. Primitive, maybe – but it works.

Crazy paving is laid in much the same way as rectangular paving, except that it is always best done on mortar points (as previously described) and will require more filling in between pieces because of their irregular shapes. You can either provide a concrete base, or work on consolidated ground. Having achieved a fairly level earth surface, well compacted, I have successfully paved after hammering rubble into the ground. Provided that the earth isn't rock hard, then the rubble goes in fairly easily and gives that extra bit of strength if concreting is thought unnecessary. While a level finish is important with smooth-surfaced crazy paving, it is not quite so critical with irregular, natural stone where a level can only be determined over larger areas in any case. Again it is sound practice to use large pieces for the edges.

MODEST WALLING

Low walls for screens, raised plant beds, raised paving, or simply to divide one part of the garden from another, are quite elementary to construct. The difficulty increases with height, not just from the point of view of building it upright but with regard to maintaining its vertical state permanently. Long, high walls, as would be required for boundary work, have to be strengthened by pillars at intervals. While not by any means beyond your grasp, they are certainly more tricky.

Low, decorative walls present few problems. They can be constructed from natural stone, artificial stone, bricks, screen blocks or a combination of materials. The depth of wall foundations, or 'footings' to use the correct term, will vary according to the stability of the ground and the weight they will have to bear. The higher the wall, the more weight, though screen blocks are relatively light in proportion to size so will exert far less pressure than the equivalent volume of brick or stone.

Generally, a foundation of concrete four to six inches deep and half as wide again as the width of the wall will be sufficient. Dig out a trench to the correct dimensions, and produce levels by the peg method described for patio and path platforms. The footings should end up at least an inch below the surface so that they will not be seen later on. Here's another opportunity to get rid of any old iron, which embedded in the concrete will increase the overall strength. Note: entombing bills or income tax demands does nothing for the wall's subsequent stability.

When using bricks or uniform size artificial stone, the traditional method of laying is adopted – that is, complete bricks never go one above the other but bridge the lower joints. This will involve you in the need for some half bricks, but don't panic – they are quite easily cut with a hammer and bolster. Personally I've never been able to master the bricklayer's art of chopping them with a trowel, but you could always try.

The first row of bricks or stones is laid on about half-an-inch of mortar, comprising three parts sand to one part cement mixture with a plasticiser added to the water. A plasticiser gives the mortar more flexibility and will help prevent cracking. Washing-up liquid added to the water improves the working time. The mixture should also be relatively dry, otherwise water squeezed out will run down the wall, leaving marks. Getting exactly the right consistency demands a bit of trial and error, because if the mixture is too dry you will have trouble levelling the bricks by tapping.

Brick laying for the complete novice can be very much a-knife-and-fork-and-grappling-with-your-fingers affair. Laying mortar on top of the last row to receive the next is no problem, but more practice is required to make that blob on the end of each brick stay put long enough to reach the wall. It mostly falls off and you end up poking mortar between the bricks by trowel. Check continually for straightness, and that the wall is upright and level in all directions. One way to do this is to use a line (string?) stretched between the bricks at either end of a row, and then match the rest to it. Another is to use the spirit level in conjunction with a long piece of wood. A good spirit level will have a secondary optic for checking the vertical accuracy, and this of course would be useful.

A single brick thickness is sufficient for most ornamental walls of three feet or so. Free standing screens will obviously be more sturdy and look better with a supporting pillar at each end, whereas walls that form a completed shape (to make a raised plant bed for example) will have their own rigidity. Be careful, though, when building earth retaining walls, because it is very easy to underestimate the strength required. Elevations of a foot or so should present no difficulty. But if you're thinking of a wall to hold back three feet of soil over even a modest area, the pressure could be many tons – and it would be wise to seek professional advice, or you risk a garden avalanche. In any case, you should leave a half brick out of the bottom course to allow for water drainage.

SCREEN BLOCKS

Screen blocks, open patterned units cast from cement aggregate, are very attractive and can be used on their own or with brick/artificial stone materials. A variety of designs are available and they are no more difficult to lay than bricks. But if used on their own to a height of more than three feet, support pillars will be needed. The manufacturers make special pre-cast ones, or you can make your own with bricks. Pre-cast pillars have grooves to accept the blocks, but to anchor block to brick pillars firmly, 'U' shaped pieces of wire should be built in between the two components. These are simply laid into the mortar, and it is not a bad idea to adopt the same principle between the blocks themselves as they are placed directly above one another rather than in the stronger overlapping formation.

A certain amount of finishing work has to be done to the wall. Once the mortar is no longer tacky, it should be scraped out slightly from between the bricks with a stick. A quarter of an inch is enough. Screen walls can then be capped with coping stones, which should overhang by about an inch each side.

Natural stone walls are built in much the same way, though the preoccupation with levels is nowhere near so great. Natural stone walls are *supposed* to be sticking out all over the place, and the main thing is to try not to get too much mortar over the wall face (and yours). Seasoned stone is always better than freshly quarried stuff, because it is weathered to a better texture; but this may be hard to come by. You might of course be lucky enough to hear of an old stone cottage or house that has been demolished, and be able to buy some stone there. The type of stone available at a reasonable price will very much depend on what is naturally available in your own area. Importing special stuff from the other end of the country would be exorbitant.

We have said little so far to help the builder of a high boundary wall, and at our level of enthusiasm it would seem pointless to attempt a crash course – which might just end in that literal result. If you know a bricklayer he might do it at weekends for you, or at least pass on sufficiently detailed first-hand knowledge on site to get you moving. But a thirty-foot wall of five feet or more in height is a formidable task for someone trying to minimise his efforts. So in all honesty we might be better to consider the project more cost-effective done by someone else, while we concentrate on the less demanding ones. Scavenging for tips is part of the unarmed gardener's routine.

FENCING

Alternative to the wall is the fence. While certainly not concrete, fences form a part of basic construction so most appropriately fit into this section.

Fences can be put up more quickly than walls and come in many forms. They are almost exclusively made of wood, the only exception I know of being a plastic variety of ranch-type fencing.

Good fencing is expensive, influenced by the price of timber. Larch-lap and cedar screens are probably two of the best, and should last for many years. Thin wooden strips, woven into panels, are more common and cheaper, but prone to damage.

Fencing requires support posts. When you buy any type of fence in panelled sections, these posts will be included in the cost of the 'run' – or the number of panels required. The section of post that will be below ground must be well treated with a preservative, such as creosote. As an alternative, short concrete or metal supports can be obtained to which the posts are bolted. Traditionally, posts appear on your side – sickening really, because your neighbour enjoys the best, uncluttered face of your new fence.

Whatever support system you use, the posts have to be firmly anchored if the fence is not to fall down in the first fresh wind. Anything over four feet should be concreted into position.

With panelled fencing it is not really practical to put all the posts in first. The system is to sink the first one, checking with a panel that it is the right depth. As a guide there should be two inches clearance top and bottom. Having made sure that the post is square with the fence line, fill the hole with concrete and force it down to avoid all air pockets.

You must now measure for the second hole, using either the panel itself or the capping strip which is normally separate. Once this excavation has been prepared, the panel can be nailed to the first post, using a couple of bricks underneath to fix round clearance. The next step is to position the second post and nail it to the free end of the panel, again checking clearance top and bottom. Fill the second post hole with concrete as before, and

check immediately that the whole section is upright in all planes. When you are satisfied that it is, support it with lengths of wood – these can be nailed to the fence top for removal once the concrete has set. All further panels are erected in the same way.

It would be incredible good fortune if the required distance is spanned with complete panels. The last one will almost certainly have to be cut. Measure the distance between the last two posts and mark the panel correspondingly. Remove the frames from the panel end and replace at the required width. The surplus fencing is then sawn off to give you a custom-made section to complete the job.

The final task will be to attach the 'gravel board' at ground level. This fills the gap between the fence and ground, and is partly buried. It is normally made of wood, but you can use more resistant material such as corrugated asbestos.

The board is fixed below each panel. The best method is to nail blocks of wood to each post directly beneath the sections; boards can then be attatched to these with nails – but don't try to nail through asbestos, as it will most likely crack. Drill holes and use nails with a large head, or add a washer.

When fencing sloping ground, the panels are placed in position so that each is slightly higher than its neighbour. Marginally longer posts may be needed in these circumstances.

MASTERING STEPS

Steps are not that difficult to construct, but not that easy to explain. Their function is a simple means of ascending or descending from one level to another other than by climbing, jumping, falling or negotiating a slope. That much is blatantly obvious, but you have to decide whether steps are worthwhile. Would their inclusion make moving about more difficult in certain circumstances? Would a gently sloping and continuous path be better than one including say, two steps, over a run of thirty feet? Would a bank be more easily conquered by a single laterally sloping path or one in zig-zag formation (the way roads are put across mountainous regions)? If there's a feasible

option, consider the advantages and disadvantages carefully before you make up your mind.

If a slope is to be stepped, the first job is to find out how many will be needed and what width each one will be. There's a straightforward method for modest barriers, which is all we shall deal with here. Flights ascending into infinity are beyond my experience and, excuse the pun, inclination.

For comfortable use, steps should be between five and six inches high. Taking this as a fundamental requirement, we must now measure the height to be scaled. This is done by knocking a wooden peg into the top of the slope, and a much longer one at the bottom. Using a length of wood to span them, and a spirit level, the large peg is driven into the ground until it levels up with the top one. The amount of wood still showing is the height of the rise and the distance between them the span to be covered. It is now possible to work out how many steps are needed and how wide each one will be. As an example, let's say the height is three feet, which would mean six steps six inches high. If the distance to be covered is eight feet, then that divided by the number of steps means that each one must be sixteen inches wide. See? Steeper slopes will have narrower treads, and there is obviously a practical limit to what can be achieved without cutting into the slope, extending the steps beyond it, or having a ladder.

The construction is, quite literally, step-by-step. We shall concentrate on using paving. The slopes must now be skimmed to a regular angle and marked out with two rows of pegs to show the position of each step or riser; in the case of the example above, sixteen inches apart. Dig out a footing for the first riser, and fill with about four inches of concrete. Once this has set, place your layer of bricks or stone on top, allowing for the thickness of the paving to make up the six-inch rise. If the paving is one and a half inches thick, then the support work must be four and a half inches deep. Excavate behind and up to the next riser position to allow for a four-inch concrete base. When this has dried, the paving can be cemented into position, overlapping the riser by about an inch and sloped fractionally forward to avoid rain-water lying on it. You can now excavate behind to provide a footing for the next riser, and carry on repeating the process until the steps are complete. The whole production is a fairly lengthy one, because each stage involves setting time for the concrete. And don't forget to keep checking the levels!

Steps can be made exclusively of bricks by much the same means. The only difference is that instead of slabs forming the treads, these are made up of bricks cemented together side on. They may also be cast from concrete, but these are not particularly attractive and involve the construction of a mould.

GARDEN POOLS

The presence of water in the garden, other than large puddles or more serious flooding, is always a nice touch. Today pools are very easily installed. The age of the concrete pool has really long since passed, and there are few advantages for adopting such a method which is time-consuming and sometimes even reluctant to hold water. By using a liner, plastic or glass fibre mould, an ornamental pool can be completed in a weekend to give many years of service. Certain liners, such as Stapelite (a synthetic rubber membrane based on butyl), are guaranteed for fifteen years and should last fifty. Cheaper materials are given anything from one to ten years.

Liners are supplied in square or rectangular sheets, but will accommodate a variety of shapes provided that they are not too complicated. Installation involves little more than digging a hole to the shape and depth needed. As a guide, the average size pool should have a shallow ledge about nine inches deep for marginal water plants and a deeper section of about eighteen inches. The shelf must be wide enough to take planting crates, and ten inches ought to be enough. Such a ledge can extend all the way round the pool or just part of it.

The simplest way of marking the pool shape is to lay out a rope or a hosepipe, adjusting it until the required size and shape

Suggested Plant Containers

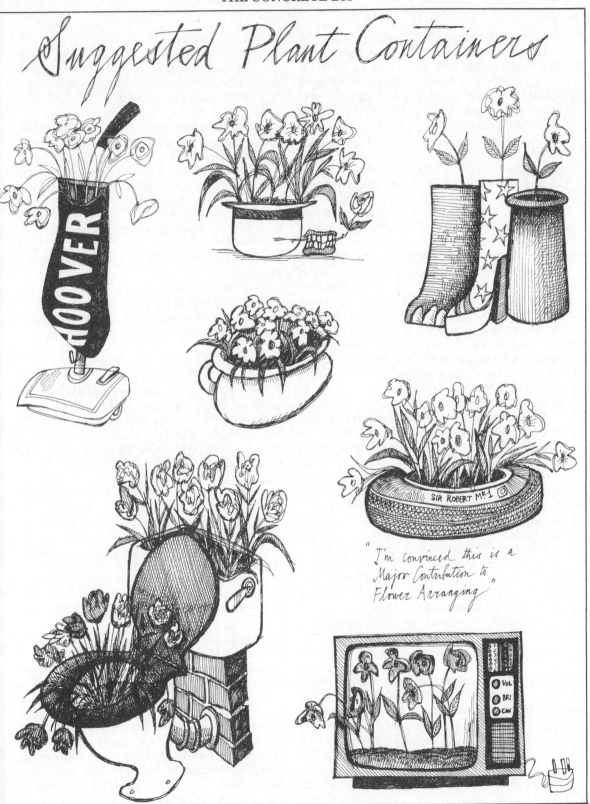

"I'm convinced this is a Major Contribution to Flower Arranging"

is achieved. Using a spade, cut out the outline – inside the marker to allow for any later trimming – after which the rope or hose can be removed. The final contours can now be excavated, sloping the sides slightly and checking to see that the pool top is level. Any protruding sharp stones should be removed and a layer of sand applied. If the ground is particularly stony, it is as well to add a precautionary layer of polythene.

The pool liner should now be draped evenly over the hole, weighted by stones at the edges. Start putting in the water which will start to drag the liner into position. Ease off the weights now and again to help it slide in evenly. Once filled with water, the liner will be pressed tightly into place by the weight of water and surplus material can be trimmed off with scissors, leaving a four- to five-inch overlap. A foot wide layer of paving can now be cemented around the edge, overhanging the pool by about two inches. If the pool is being excavated into an existing lawn, provision should be made for the final paving so that it ends up below the grass level, to make mowing easier.

Pre-formed pools are laid in much the same way, a hole being dug to accept the shape but slightly larger. The base is compacted and a layer of sand added. Once the pool is in position, start filling in around it with more sand and adding water as you go. Special care must be taken to ensure that the shelves are amply supported. Stone edging is then added as before.

Plants will be needed to put oxygen into the water, but should not be added until after the water has stood for a couple of days. They are first planted in plastic containers lined with hessian and topped with a layer of fine gravel. They won't look at all spectacular to start with and are generally supported on bricks until they become larger and well established. Your actual fish can go in two weeks after the plants, though concrete pools must be specially treated before anything live is introduced. How many fish you have depends on the size of the pool and the size of the fish. Work it out as two inches of fish for every square foot of surface water. Thirty square feet will take thirty two-inch fish, or fifteen four-inch fish and so on – but *not* one

five-foot specimen ...

A great range of fish can be bought, from the familiar Goldfish to Shubunkin, Golden Orfe, Comet Longtails, Black Moors and Green Tench. The Japanese Nishiki Koi Carp is a spectacular addition to larger pools. In lakes, they can reach three feet in length!

Fountains can help turn a mere pool into a water garden. The simplest system is a submersible pump to which a fountain jet can be attached. Fountains not only look attractive but have the added benefit of oxygenating the water, which is good news for the fish. Waterfalls can also be added, as can underwater lighting to produce that really spectacular effect. Maintenance aids are legion.

Ornamental pools can be built above the ground, contained by walling and supported inside by earth or sand. Formal shaped pools are more suited to this arrangement.

ROCK GARDENS

A familiar feature close to pools is the rock garden. Don't confuse rock gardens with rockeries, which nine times out of ten look like, and are, a heap of stones. The secret of the real thing is to make the feature look like a natural outcrop of rock. The only way of achieving this is to study the real, real thing, and so place your stones to result in a passable imitation. Nothing looks worse than neat squares or circles: you might as well stick a gnome on it to complete such an atrocity. It is my fervent hope that one day all garden gnomes will come to life, be so appalled by the endless fishing, grinning, occupation of toadstools and so on, that they will migrate back to the pages of fairy tale books where they belong.

Rock gardens are most effective on sloping ground, which is why they make such a suitable background to pools. The type of stone will depend on cost and whatever is most prevalent in your area. Surface stone is always better because it will be weathered and etched by wind and water; it will always be more expensive, too. Large pieces are required, anything up to two hundredweight being manageable with the aid of levers. Much more than that demands bionics, a team of slaves, or comes with a free surgical support.

Popular materials include sandstone, Welsh limestone, Derby spar, and, best of all, Westmoreland. Carriage and scarcity control prices, so local stone will generally be cheaper. Small features will not shock you too much, but larger ones might run into several tons and produce a three-figure bill. And the quantities needed are enlarged by the fact that to look natural, as much as two-thirds of any one piece might have to be buried.

Rock garden sites should generally be well drained and sunny, though you can always get something to grow in them. Starting from the bottom, holes large enough to accommodate the pieces are dug and the stone then levered into position. If the stone has an obvious grain, then all pieces should match up in this respect. Further lumps are added until the feature is complete – with loads of pockets that can be filled with soil and planted. On a flat site, where they can add some much needed height to the scene, stones will probably be placed closer together and built up. These constructions seldom appear so natural as sloping features, but the whole thing is very much up to your creative ability and 'feel' for the subject. You'll certainly feel your back the next morning.

CONTAINERS

Large, paved areas need some relief whenever it is impossible to incorporate spaces for plants. This is where the container comes into its own. Containers provide the key to a flexible garden. Just as you might move the furniture around in your house, for a change, so it is possible to modify the garden by shuffling containers full of flowers, shrubs, a tree, and so on.

Containers themselves can be almost anything that will hold soil and which is small enough to manhandle. There are those who revel in having the most unusual device. One garden I recall specialised in using old toilets for floral features, though the enthusiast did not logically expand the scheme to embrace a cistern and chain for flush watering.

If decorated thunderboxes are not your scene, then what about an old wheelbarrow, boots, chimney pot, two halves of a barrel, pig trough, cauldron, coal scuttle, primitive stone kitchen sink, bucket, even a redundant telephone kiosk? The possibilities are endless, and it's largely up to your ingenuity to adapt a seemingly unlikely subject into a garden attraction.

On the other hand, a vast range of manufactured containers is on tap, none of which could be easily mistaken for a WC or a wheelbarrow. They come in modern or traditional designs, might be made from stone or plastic, and in some cases are treated to appear ancient.

Whatever form of container you use, it must have a few drainage holes at the bottom to prevent waterlogging. To set one up, place a layer of broken pots or similar coarse debris in the bottom. Next add ordinary garden soil to about a third of the depth. Top layer must be compost, so display great knowledge at the nearest garden centre by asking for the required quantity of 'John Innes Number 3'. The required volume must be estimated on the spot from the sizes of available bags.

After a good watering, plants can be introduced, annual bedding material going in during June. This might include geraniums, fuchsias, petunias, salvias, allysum, lobelia and so on. When these have finished, you can re-plant with wallflowers or spring bulbs such as daffodils, dwarf tulips, snowdrops, hyacinths or muscari.

Permanent plants won't give as much colour but are effective as foliage features. Good subjects include dwarf conifers, heathers, and dwarf evergreens.

All container grown plants will require feeding, particularly permanent ones, as the natural nourishment will rapidly be depleted. Any proprietary general feed will do, used according to the instructions.

This really concludes the basics of concrete gardening, with a bit of stone and water thrown in. The results are as permanent as can reasonably be expected and will certainly last longer than your car, even though the life of that might be slightly extended due to the extra time you will be able to give it. But unarmed car maintenance is another story!

4. The Green Bit

'Those about to die salute you' was the ritualistic rather than sincere address made by gladiators to chief dignitaries attending Imperial Rome's equivalent of *It's a Knock-out.* For all we know plants may communicate the same resigned message as they are committed to the arena we call a garden.

Past experience may well make you especially sympathetic to such a theory. But we have selected a stronger squad this time, with our Survivors (see also Chapter Two) more evenly matched against the champion weeds. (I've never been able to reconcile the term 'weedy' with the implications of a puny stature – perhaps it's an extravagance of opposite meaning, in the same way that enormous people are called Tiny or Slim.)

While our challengers can take care of themselves, this Green Bit chapter will not only deal with non-concrete construction but also see if plants can be given an extra edge – without us getting too carried away, of course.

In sheer surface area, lawns are almost certainly the largest green construction job. But making a lawn to the unpretentious standard we require is child's play (that's a thought ...), needing no special skill: just effort, in preparing the ground. There are two methods of lawn creation – from seed or turf. Turf is always more appealing, because the lawn is instant as far as superficial appearance goes. Impatience is always the sign of a non-gardener.

We'll save the best bit until last, and study first the preparation of ground for a seeded lawn.

LAWNS FROM SEED

Assuming the site is currently a disgrace, it must first be cleared of weeds, large pieces of rubble, old car bodies, people who have become lost etc. Surface debris can be picked up and the area dug or rotovated. If the undergrowth is particularly dense, it would be easier to spray with what is known as a 'total non-residual herbicide', in other words a weed-killer which is active in contact with vegetation but is neutralised in the soil. Digging starts once the weeds have died down.

Once cultivation is complete, the whole area must be raked roughly level and broken down to a fine texture. In dry conditions, stones can be raked out as part of that process. Particularly poor ground, where a lot of sub-soil has been brought to the surface by building works, would be better covered by imported top soil. A good six-inch covering is advisable. The whole area must now be firmed, an operation popularly termed 'consolidating by treading'. If you think that means walking about all over it, you're just about right – but the firming is done with all your weight on one heel. This method is surprisingly effective at producing a uniform packing, but indescribably boring. Now the surface is raked again to a fine finish and any outstanding, localised levelling done.

At this stage a little help can be given to the prospective lawn by applying a suitable fertiliser. I won't bore you with the ingredients, just ask for the right ready-mixed stuff at your local garden centre. It must be added at least ten days before seeding or turfing.

The time for sowing grass seed is between April and October, avoiding prolonged rainless periods or cold, wet ones. Ideal conditions are wet and warm. If the weather is dry, then quite a lot of watering will be necessary if the seed is to germinate quickly and develop. A fine spray is needed to avoid washing the seed right away or into concentrations.

The general density of grass seed is two ounces per square yard, though this proportion is not critical. The less seed, the longer the lawn will take to thicken, that's all. Seed is cast by hand to save buying special equipment, and to help even distribution the plot can be divided off into one yard squares. Afterwards the seed is lightly raked into the surface, though half of it is likely to remain on top. This is not a problem; what will be of concern is that apart from starting a lawn you have simultaneously laid out a sumptuous feast for every bird in the neighbourhood. It is quite amazing how quickly the word gets round about a new diner opening, and eager beaks will soon be queuing up to go through the card.

Some seed is treated with a repellent, alleged by the sarcastic to be an extract from British Rail sausage rolls. A degree of protection from winged marauders can be offered by a few strings of milk bottle tops on sticks that will rattle in the wind. Keeping animals off is more difficult, though startling effects are claimed for one or two products on the market. A powdered deterrent I once tried showed a cat and a dog fleeing in stark terror. Whatever was behind them to cause such a dramatic and unconditional retreat might well be of great interest to the Ministry of Defence. It certainly wasn't the potion, which, if anything, attracted more animals than usual and almost got our own cat addicted. On reflection, it seems that the stuff might have worked if placed at a point as far as possible from the area to be protected, thereby luring assorted varmints away.

Lawn seed is not comprised of just one variety. Various grasses are mixed to suit specific requirements, such as the quality of finished lawn and the type of soil. A general purpose mixture to suit dry conditions, for example, might contain such marvellously named varieties as Creeping Red Fescue, Chewings Fescue, Perennial Ryegrass and Crested Dogs Tail. Wet situations might have a helping of Rough Stalked Meadow Grass instead of the Crested Dogs Tail. Really hard-wearing lawns should be dominated by Perennial Ryegrass supported by a drop of the old Dogs Tail and Smooth Stalked Meadow Grass. Packaged mixtures can be bought to suit your needs, and it's best to seek expert advice at the garden centre or wherever the seed is stocked.

First mowing can be carried out when the grass is about two inches high, the mower being set to take about half-an-inch off. This height can be lowered gradually as the grass becomes more strongly established. Cutting and rolling helps to stimulate auxiliary growth by bruising the stems.

LAWNS FROM TURF
The preparation of the site for a turfed lawn is basically the same as for the seeded variety, except that we need not be quite so fussy about the state of the surface so long as it is relatively flat. Small stones will not be a problem as the turf will cover all these.

There is no major reason why turf should

not be laid at any time of the year, except when either the ground is likely to remain frozen, or under drought conditions when there are likely to be restrictions on the use of water.

Cheap turf is seldom good value, because under normal conditions turf takes two years of cultivation to the point of sale. It should be almost totally free of weeds and the pieces ought to be of the same thickness, otherwise a lot of time will be spent underpacking with soil to achieve a uniform level. Turf is generally sold by the square yard, so you'll have to estimate the area to be covered. Don't forget to allow for curves and any flower beds to be sited within the grassed area.

Before laying your turf, water the ground well if it is dry. Then lay out one edge of the lawn, pulling the pieces of turf together with the back of a rake and then using the flat part to firm each piece down. To lay the next row, place a plank on the first section to stand on, avoiding making depressions in the still softish ground. Continue in the same manner, pulling the pieces together so that the joins do not show, and trimming off any ragged pieces with a penknife. It is not really necessary to bond turf like brickwork, since the sections will soon knit together if they are kept well watered. Allowing freshly laid turf to dry out will result in shrinkage, and the grass may even die since its only source of water, until the roots have taken, is from above.

Stay off your new lawn for a couple of weeks, and adopt the same mowing principles as with seed. Don't use weedkillers in the first season, but a fertiliser can be applied six weeks after the roots have struck. There's no doubt that turf has tremendous appeal because many of the problems associated with seed simply don't apply. And best of all, one day it's not there, the next it is ... and the next it isn't, if someone pinches it, which is not unknown. One consolation is that to have your lawn stolen is a great item of conversational one-upmanship.

TREES AND SHRUBS
Now let's have a go at planting a tree or a shrub. These can be bought either in con-
tainers or bare-rooted. Container-grown plants are a great aid to the impatient novice, since they can be installed at virtually any time of the year and are frequently bought with flowers in bloom so that it's possible to see exactly what you're getting. Those sold 'nude' are in their dormant period and have a planting span which stretches between November and March. Neither are committed to the earth when it is frozen; it's hard work to dig, apart from what the plants might think about such treatment.

Containers might be plastic, pot, felt or whalehide. The latter does not even have to be removed as it will rot away in the ground. Plastic and pot containers must be detached, but provided the soil within is moist and a good root system has developed, little disturbance is caused. Plastic bag containers are cut away; solid pots are inverted and tapped at the bottom until the plant, complete with soil, slides out.

The receiving hole needs to be slightly larger than the roots-plus-soil, and the gaps filled with loose soil once the plant is in position. This portion should be firmed with the heel, but don't go and crush the root ball. Alternatively, as an aid to growth, part of the hole can be filled with moist peat topped by a mixture of soil, peat and bonemeal. Always ensure that the final soil level matches up with the original in the container, and water regularly in dry weather.

Trees and shrubs bought bare rooted (many roses are sold in this way) need a little more care. The hole needs to be large enough to accept the spread-out roots and the bottom is loosened up with a fork. Soil, or peat, is then filtered between the roots and the hole finally topped up. The soil/peat/bonemeal mixture will again help boost the plant's prospects, and the same ritual of firming is performed.

Young trees will need supporting with a stake, which is driven into position *before planting* to avoid doing an anti-vampire job on the roots. Suitable stakes and ties can often be bought as part of a kit with the trees. Old drainpipes and bits of string don't exactly enhance appearance.

When positioning, bear in mind the final size of the plant. It's obviously pointless to have an enormous shrub somewhere in the foreground which will hide everything behind it and probably obstruct the path. And don't expect to go out and buy fully mature specimens. You can, but they will cost a fortune, and the slower the rate of growth the more expensive they will be. (Inevitably.)

HEDGES AND SCREENS

Hedges and screens are much the same thing, though it is common to think of one as a boundary barrier and the other as a more loosely connected divider. A hedge is just a row of shrubs planted closely together so that they eventually intermingle and appear as one. Privet is probably the most common, being fast growing, cheap, very competitive and mostly evergreen. Plants are best placed eighteen inches apart in two, staggered rows, three inches apart. Hedges generally need well fertilised ground because they are densely planted, and privet particularly has a tremendous appetite. Well in advance of planting, dig out a foot-deep trench and put in manure or compost mixed with bonemeal. The trench can be completely re-filled with a mixture of soil, peat and bonemeal. That sounds a bit fiddly, but the extra effort will make our hedge grow that bit faster.

Popular alternatives to privet are laurel, which is evergreen with large glossy leaves in greens and yellows; and beech, extremely attractive with leaves that change in colour during the season. Beech is not an evergreen shrub, but the brown leaves in autumn generally remain until fresh ones appear in spring to give a permanent shield. Green beech can be mixed with its copper cousin to provide variety.

All three varieties can be shaped as they mature with shears, or a hedge-trimmer in the case of privet and beech – but use secateurs for laurel, because a lot of large leaves cut in half don't look so good.

Many shrubs and conifers will make informal screens where trimming is not necessary until the desired height has been reached. For those wanting quick results, the king of vigorous conifers goes by the twenty-four letter name of *cupressocyparis leylandii*

(there's no common title and it has nothing to do with British Leyland). On full noise this tree machine can grow well over two feet a year. Initially it may look rather straggly, but will eventually become more bushy. Bare-rooted conifers are planted in May or September as described earlier.

CLIMBING PLANTS

Climbing plants will also make a screen if there is something to cling to in the first place, such as trellis panels or a framework of rustic poles. They will also adorn bare walls or fences. Most frequently seen are roses, clematis and honeysuckle, which appears under the family title *lonicera*, if you get stuck on names. These varieties will be quite small when bought, probably in a container and demonstrating their climbing habit by hanging off a short stick. It is wise to seek on-the-spot advice about numbers of plants required, depending on choice of plant. Certain clematis, such as Montana, will rapidly put on about thirty feet of growth and provide a very dense covering. You obviously wouldn't need many of those to smother a support. Clematis often do better if their roots are well shaded. Flat pieces of stone around the base of the plant will often suffice.

All climbers need a little help at the start to get them growing in the right direction. The extending shoots should be loosely tied to produce an even covering and avoid overlapping. When the plants are fully established, you will have to maintain control by shortening outward growing shoots, trimming the height and taking out dead wood which might clog the plant.

In a very sheltered position you might succeed with the spectacular Passion Flower. I experimented with a single plant which for two years stubbornly refused to make any progress at all and if anything got smaller. Then over a period of two seasons, and without any aid from me, it ran amok, covering sixty square feet of wall. You can actually stand and watch the flowers opening and though they only last about forty-eight hours, a succession of hundreds were produced. This creation is now starting to invade the house next door, competing with a

previously dominant clematis. So far it looks like a survivor; the terrifying thing is it might have a go at something more ambitious.

PERMANENT BULBS

Bulbs are useful devices in that they can mostly be left in the ground to look after themselves. You're not supposed to, but in my experience things like daffodils, crocuses and snowdrops keep coming up every year regardless. And while the flowers might be slightly smaller than those dried and rested for a few months each year, the overall effect is much the same.

If permanent interment is the case, there's not a lot to say about bulbs. Generally they look better in groups rather than regimented lines, and it's also easier to remember where they are. Since for much of the year there will be no visible signs of presence, it is easy to ravage concealed bulbs in a fit of enthusiasm for rough forking or hoeing. The only concession mine get is decapitation of dead flowers, as this allows the bulb to concentrate energy into itself rather than producing a seed head. This is one of the reasons why spectacular displays of tulip fields are now rarely seen in Lincolnshire. Not that I flash about chopping the flowers off myself you understand – the growers do, to develop the bulb and make decorated floats for an annual parade.

Spring flowering bulbs are planted from the beginning of September to the end of December. They go in about a three-inch hole, the sharp end pointing upwards. Also among the range are snowdrops, crocuses, narcissus and dwarf irises, all good lurkers waiting to grow once a year.

Gladioli are fairly simple to operate, and planting of corms can start at the end of March. They should be put in about six inches down, and will flower in summer and early autumn depending on when you planted them. Anemones are treated just about the same and there are scores of other bulbs/corms/tubers that you could dabble with. But so many need storing at some stage that our long-term labour-saving objective would quickly be defeated.

BEDDING PLANTS

Bedding plants are a bit of a nuisance, but small areas don't cause too much aggravation and will give patches of strong colour. The easiest way is to choose those that can be grown from seed sown directly into the ground. Such specimens go under the classification of 'hardy annuals' and you might consider marigolds, candytuft, clarkia, cornflower, godetia, larkspur, poppies and night-scented stocks. These can be committed from mid-March to the end of April, scattering seeds over the prepared ground and then lightly raking them in. The best effects are created by massed plants of the same type, though they should be thinned out at seedling stage – assuming enough survive bird raids to make this necessary. Some form of frightener is handy to deter all but the boldest bird – there's always one with nerves of steel and a bionic beak.

The next easiest way, but also the most expensive, is to buy bedding plants ready for setting out in the garden. They are most commonly purchased by the tray and must then be separated for individual planting. This is not too bad for the first ten minutes but gets progressively more tedious. As a general rule, six inches apart is about right. The soil needs to be damp, so that it can be firmed around the small plants and of course achieve good penetration of fingernails.

A more enthusiastic method is to grow the plants yourself in seed trays or pots. Should you have an unheated greenhouse then the seeds can be sown in moist compost from mid-March or on a window-sill around mid-April. They can be covered with glass to retain moisture, and specific instructions will be on the seed packet. Likely subjects are dahlias, marigolds, asters, stocks, petunias, nicotiana, alyssum, zinnias, phlox and rudbeckia, all of which are common enough.

There is always a good chance of obtaining free bedding plants from a friendly, more thrusting gardener who has grown more than he can possibly find space for. Be on the lookout for these opportunities. Praising other people's Green Bits can often encourage dividends, so you'll know what they're after when someone goes into ecstasies over yours, won't you?

5. The Vegetable & Fruit Bit

If civilisation as we know it ended tomorrow, how long would I last? That's a question frequently pondered, and my answer always indicates that I'd be one of the first to go in a free-for-all at basic levels of survival. All I remember from a session in the Boy Scouts is how to tie a washing line together, and how to cripple the stomach with imitation bread on the end of a stick. I didn't like camping either.

The possessor of such pathetically inadequate skills could scarcely expect to become a leader among fellow strugglers. Some people I know can catch fish without actually getting in there and grappling with them; others can shoot fowl and do all the necessary nasty bits afterwards; more can join pieces of wood together to resemble a useful item.

So for someone who has led a sheltered life, inspired only by the materialistic things that money can buy and ignoring realities that money can avoid, the prospects in a pioneer world are less than encouraging. But in the Vegetable and Fruit Bit we can, with a little courage, tentatively span the dual realities of existence. One involves succeeding within the standing rules, and the other requires continued participation if the game changes.

It is the slight overlap between these two things that we shall be looking at – which simply means offering a home-grown thing to a mass-produced and technically baffling means of cooking it. We shall not suddenly become satisfyingly self-sufficient, only sufficiently self-satisfied in having brought something to the table other than an appetite.

The description 'vegetables and fruit' covers a vast range of edibles from the common potato to such exotica as pineapples. Only those most easily grown will be dealt with and our standards are modest. The ultimate crop demands the ultimate skill and effort. With luck and a little judgement, we shall conspire to achieve passable offerings in blissful ignorance of the more profound advice available.

VEGETABLES

The prospective menu will start with vegetables, which can be principally divided into those that grow in the ground (potatoes, carrots, beetroot etc) and those that develop above the ground (peas, beans, cabbages and the like). Arguably there are some that grow half in and half out but that's too fine a point on which to dwell.

POTATOES

Of all in-ground produce (root crops), potatoes must take first place. The versatile spud can be boiled, roasted, baked, fried into a chip or crisp and reduced to dehydrated form for instant mash. In between are variations and adaptations too numerous to mention and difficult to spell. Thankfully, growing the raw material is much less diversified and well within our grasp.

As I'm sure you know, potatoes are grown from other potatoes, re-classified as seed potatoes. They are somewhat special, in that what you plant is a replica of what you hope to dig up. You can't, after all, plant a parsnip to grow into other parsnips in quite the same way.

It is reassuring to note that millions of tons of potatoes are successfully grown in Britain every year, and the current record yield from just six potatoes is an incredible 1800 pounds. The techniques necessary to perform such a miracle of productivity are expensive, time-absorbing and, to some extent, closely guarded secrets. One aspect is 'layering', which involves the pegging down of foliage to produce satellite roots.

Potatoes are divided into the categories earlies, second earlies, and lates (main crop). Earlies are planted in late March and should be ready for eating in thirteen weeks. Second earlies have about the same development time but go in around mid-April. Lates can be planted in April or May, but take longer to reach maturity, generally seventeen to twenty weeks. They need a little more room and should be installed five inches down, fifteen inches apart, in rows thirty inches apart. Earlies require separations of twelve inches and twenty-four inches.

For best results, a rich soil is necessary – so you might feel inclined to buy a bag of fertiliser. It also pays to invest in good seed, which mostly originates from Scotland and Ireland. A little growing time is saved if the seed has shoots up to one inch long. These point upwards when planting and some schools of thought recommend breaking off all but the two strongest shoots.

When foliage is about six inches high, you can make those nice V-shaped formations by drawing earth up with a hoe from between the rows and up to the stems. However, this is not done to improve appearance but to reduce moisture loss, and to keep the foliage fairly upright; it also makes handy watering trenches and covers developing potatoes to prevent them turning green and poisonous.

Early crops can be harvested after an exploratory probe reveals potatoes large enough to eat. Lates should be left until the foliage, or 'haulm' to use the technical term, has begun to die down. When lifting, make your fork approach well away from the plant to minimise the risk of spiking potatoes. Casual thrusting will wreak great havoc – unless the potatoes are too small to hit, of course.

It is generally recommended that old potato foliage is burned and not put on a compost heap, where it might perpetuate disease. The same applies to any infected material from other plants.

CARROTS AND PARSNIPS

Nothing could be more simple than carrots. Seeds can be sown direct into the garden in half-inch deep 'grooves' set a foot apart. Spread the seed fairly thinly and as evenly as possible. Do it on a calm day otherwise the things will go everywhere except the intended slot, and to achieve a good flow, stagger sowing from March to July. There's no point in having all your carrots ready at the same time.

When the seedlings are about three inches tall, they should be thinned out to around three inches apart. It's a bit sickening to have to pull up something that you've got to grow, but such is the merciless nature of carrot growing. Eating time is up to you, but try to let them put on a bit of weight first; have a look at them after about eight weeks, depending on the weather.

Parsnips, which look like frightened carrots, are grown in much the same way. But these blanched roots take longer to develop. Sow in March and thin out to about nine inches apart. They don't mind frost, and so can be left in the ground over the winter to be plucked as required.

BEETROOT

The popular salad component, beetroot, is another easy one. Seeds can be scattered in one-and-a-half-inch deep drills fifteen inches apart from late April through to May, with perhaps a second shot in June to provide later supplies. Some seed (not just beetroot) may be pelleted, that is covered with a substance which breaks down after sowing. This makes it easier to distribute seed evenly and eliminates much of the thinning out.

Beetroot need plenty of water to stay tender, but also have a weakness for going to seed, or bolting. The foliage starts to shoot upwards but if the root is lifted as soon as symptoms appear, it should be OK to eat. Those left to run amok will be woody. Beetroot is one vegetable that likes its condiments while growing rather than on the plate. A maritime plant, our purple charge will relish some common salt spread over the planting site at about one ounce to the square yard. Be careful not to wound the root when lifting, because beet bleeds and will turn pale when pickled, losing much of its flavour. And twist the leaves off rather than cutting, because this also reduces bleeding.

RADISHES

Still on salads, the humble radish is elementary, being sown in quarter-inch deep drills set six inches apart from early March to July. The quicker they grow the better they'll be, so keep well watered and apply some fertiliser before sowing.

TURNIPS

Going up in size, turnips are no real bother, early varieties being sown half an inch down in rows one foot apart from February to May. Late ones go in during June and July. They should be thinned to about six inches apart and kept free of weeds. Earlies can be lifted when still quite young, while lates must come up in October.

ONIONS AND SHALLOTS

Onions might be grown from seed or sets. The latter must be easier, so plant the small bulbs out during March or April with the tops just protruding. The relevant distances are six inches apart, in rows one foot apart. Lifting takes place in September when the onions should be dried and then stored in trays somewhere cool and dry.

Shallots, smashing for pickling if your digestion can cope, are planted from February onwards in exactly the same way as for onions. They will be ready when the leaves start to turn yellow, probably in July. Dry out and store in trays until required.

Birds are particularly fascinated by the green growing tips of onions and shallots. They have an infuriating habit of pulling them out of the ground, which means you have to go and stick them back in again. This battle to see who gets fed up first generally continues until the bulbs have rooted or disappeared altogether.

LEEKS

There's a fair variety of greens you can hazard, and among these are leeks. To save fiddling about, buy young leeks for planting in July. They go in holes made with a dibber, often resembling a sawn-off spade handle with a point on the end – though any suitable probe will do. Two or three inches of plant should show above the surface but don't fill the holes in, just fill with water. Rows should be fifteen inches apart, and the plants nine inches. In September, soil can be drawn around the leeks to blanch the stems, and harvesting can commence from November onwards as required.

CABBAGES

If cabbages are your particular fetish, these can be available all year round as any caterpillar with a spark of determination knows. They are almost impossible to fail with – all the least appetising things are – and can be grown from seed, or from young plants purchased at the appropriate time.

The right time for committing young spring cabbages is September/October;

summer types, March/June; winter versions, June/July. Instal them firmly, generally around eighteen inches apart, water well, and keep the spaces in between well hoed. Cut when the heads are firm.

BRUSSELS SPROUTS

Brussels sprouts take up space for a long period, which can't be bad, so are well worth trying. Again it's easier, though more expensive, to buy seedling sprouts to plant out in April to May, about thirty inches apart. The soil must be kept firm around the plants to give them stability as altitude and weight increases. By early autumn, sprouts of about one-inch diameter can be snapped off and any decayed leaves removed. Cropping takes place over a long period and if two, staggered plantings are made you can still be picking early the next spring, provided that seasonal varieties are chosen.

Cauliflowers are far less predictable, and so are not recommended for the unarmed gardener.

RUNNER BEANS

However, we can approach beans with confidence. Runner beans are one of my favourites and a fun vegetable to grow since they form a colourful – and edible – screen in the garden, apparent from several doors away. Runners can be sown in the intended site during May. Or, if you have a greenhouse, everything can be advanced by inserting into pots in early April. Alternatively you can always buy seedlings when needed.

For runner beans, a climbing frame has to be built, or bought. If doing your own then canes are the answer, the basic shape being an inverted 'V' formation. Each bean needs an ascender and these can be either more canes or string. Beans or plants need to be separated by ten inches in rows at least twelve inches apart. The frame obviously corresponds to these measurements. Since not all beans are guaranteed to survive through defect or slugs, it is as well to have a few extra for replacements.

The bean plants will happily climb the height of the frame, at which point the tips should be pinched out to stop upward growth. Brilliant red flowers will, you hope, be replaced by actual beans, which can be harvested as required – always pick the largest ones first. If allowed to grow too large, they will become very stringy and inedible, but impressive nonetheless.

DWARF FRENCH BEANS

If support frames are too much bother, have a go at dwarf French beans which taste much the same as runners but lie about all over the ground – though they can be supported with odd twigs and things. Seeds can be set in open ground late April/early May, spaced six inches apart in rows eighteen inches distant. Pods should be picked regularly while in their youth for best results.

BROAD BEANS

Broad beans are a hardy species and can be applied in three sowings for sustained availability. Main crop broad beans are introduced as early as February, but can continue into April. For later yields sow in July or, for a spring crop, pop them in during November. The planting depth is two inches, beans to be two inches apart within double rows ten inches apart. Allow a further two feet between each double row. All this measuring will drive you mad, but most of it can be estimated since precision planting is neither essential nor totally practicable.

Pods should be picked while young to provide the most succulent dishes. To help ward off blackfly, the great curse of broad beans, pinch out the growing tips when plants are in full flower.

Peas are not recommended because they take up too much space in relation to the likely yield from minimum effort.

MARROWS

Marrows can hardly fail to fascinate even the most reluctant gardener, the largest possible specimen being a great status symbol and a target to beat the next year. Marrow boasting is common enough, always adding on a couple of inches for prospective growth both in length and girth. Exact weight is difficult to claim or deny until the monster is actually cut (e.g. harvested).

To grow an enormous marrow you will need to dig in plenty of manure or compost, you must never allow the plants to dry out, and you must feed with fertiliser at the first signs of weakening.

Seeds can be set out in the prepared site from mid-May, two feet apart for bush varieties and three feet for trailing models. Young beasts can be chopped off as required, but select a few to be fully expanded which are cut in late September, when the skins are ripened hard, for storage somewhere cool but protected from frost. These are the big ones to prompt gasps of amazement from those yet to experience the creation of vegetable leviathans.

LETTUCE
Now back to salads, and something more mundane: lettuce is a must. Seed can be sown outside from early March and continued at fortnightly intervals until July for successive crops. Drills should be a foot apart and half-an-inch deep. When thinning to approximately ten inches apart, some of the discarded seedlings can be used to make a further row or two and these will mature slightly later. Plenty of water is essential, and use as soon as they are ready to prevent bolting. You'll soon be sick of the sight of lettuce.

TOMATOES
Successful tomato growing outdoors depends very much on the weather. Getting loads of green ones isn't a problem, advancing to the reddened stage is what causes disappointment. Such failure is often due to setting the plants out too early, which retards growth. Hardened young plants can be set out at the end of May or early June in the most sunny position available. They can go into the ground or, as is increasingly popular, into plastic bags filled with growing compound. The benefit of bags is that they can be placed on a section of path or patio, utilising tamed space.

Plants can be raised from seed if you have a heated greenhouse, but they are also readily bought. The correct planting distance is eighteen inches apart, and each needs a four-foot cane for support. The plant is tied loosely to the cane as it grows. All side shoots must be removed; these appear at the junction of main stem and leaf stalks. Tomatoes need plenty of water regularly and a liquid feed should be added every two weeks after the first fruit appears. Pinch out the top shoot four or five inches above the third truss of tomatoes to stop further upward growth.

Bush varieties need neither support nor chopping off of parts. They are perhaps most suitable for growing in bags on paving, since a cane will not hold firmly in the depth of soil available and no other means of attachment may be feasible. If the bags are placed on earth then canes can simply be pushed through.

Pick the fruit as soon as it is ripe, to give the others more chance to develop. It is best to seek advice on varieties according to whether you want a heavy cropping type or something more special. There are those that will produce vast quantities of tomatoes but generally with very little flavour. My contact recommends Outdoor Girl, Gardener's Delight, Ailsa Craig, and Sweet 100; while for bush types, Pixie, Sigmabush and Sleaford Abundance are favoured.

FRUIT
A dabble at fruit growing can often be rewarding and if you limit your efforts to simple subjects, then it need not involve too much hard labour. The size of your garden is the prime, governing factor. If space is limited then don't think in terms of huge trees and bushes; go for smaller more compact specimens that won't threaten any sort of horticultural coup.

We're not going out to win prizes, so just a small selection here will suffice for now, explained in the most basic way practicable. It could be that success – or failure – will prompt a quest for more detailed knowledge, in which case you may wish to invest in a specialist book. This will either solve your problems, confuse you even more or put you off the idea altogether. There are some quite fiendish means of making things grow that are best left to those with keener interest.

APPLES, PLUMS AND PEARS

Apples and pears make fair subjects, and are available in dwarf form as well as full size. Miniatures can also be grown in tubs, scattered about patio areas or paths. But they can be peculiar in terms of pollination and it is mostly necessary to accommodate more than one variety. They must also be compatible, and this less embarrassing aspect of birds and bees education may be freely discussed with your supplier.

By far the best time for planting, and this applies to all fruit trees, bushes and canes – excluding strawberries – is early autumn. If necessary you can get stuck in during the winter when conditions are not arctic, but don't leave it later than early spring. Trees need a good start so it's as well to buy a bit of peat and fertiliser to cast into the holes with them. At least it eases the conscience. Support stakes will be necessary to stop them blowing over or working loose.

Plums are quite popular and some will look after their own pollination. Nevertheless, crops are mostly better if another variety is present. The same applies to cherries, where particularly recommended is Amber Heart because of its great reliability. Planting methods are the same as for apples and pears.

By exercising the pruner's art, pears and plums can be made to grow in fan shapes against sunny walls while apples and pears make good cordon subjects, being planted at forty-five degree angles two or three feet apart. Basically the trees are encouraged to grow 'flat' by training and/or removing outward sprouting parts. Fans need an artistic eye to get the best shape, while cordons merely have to fill in the vertical plane between themselves. This whole thing can be a fiddly business requiring lots of support canes and wire in the formative stages, but the effect and produce is very good if you fancy your chances. Best look for more detailed instructions, or better still, find a local ace for on-the-spot tuition. He might even do it for you, just to show off.

CURRANTS AND GOOSEBERRIES

Of bush fruits, we might risk blackcurrants, redcurrants and gooseberries. For ease of access they should be planted about five feet apart and again will appreciate whatever soil nourishment or improvement that can be offered at the time. If one section of the garden is to be graced by bushes then it's not a bad idea to prepare the entire area in advance, working in any well-rotted manure or compost that comes your way (hopefully not thrown).

Blackcurrant bushes will probably be about two years old when bought. They should go in slightly deeper than the existing soil level mark, perhaps with three or four buds buried. Now comes the silly bit – chop all the branches off to about an inch above the ground, just above the last buds showing on each stem.

Though blackcurrants fruit on both young and old wood, fresh stuff provides the better crop. So regular attacks with the secateurs are necessary, the purpose being to inspire as much new growth as possible. Only remove weak, spindly bits the first winter after fruiting, but subsequently around a third of the growth can be taken out, always victimising old parts and trying to keep the centre open. This can be done as soon as the last fruit has been picked.

Redcurrants require less radical mutilation and after planting have all branches cut back to half their length to the nearest outward pointing bud. New growth is treated in the same way for the next three years, after which only the tips of shoots need amputating, at the same time controlling sideways growth. More vigorous purges are justified if development of new wood is slow.

Prickly gooseberry bushes are better defended against the pruning iron and should be treated gingerly. New bushes are savaged after planting by chopping off all but the four most muscular branches, which are themselves reduced to a quarter of their original length. For the next couple of years, main branches are halved, weak ones and sideways shoots cut back to one bud. For general tidiness modify overlapping branches, ones that droop to the ground, and also do a little summer clip on sideshoots.

A SPOT-THE-GREENHOUSE CONTEST

ADAM

Apart from birds, your most formidable garden enemy might be the local scrumping expert. One side of my redcurrant bushes at a previous abode was regularly decimated by an unknown enthusiast. They always disappeared close to a panelled fence which ran alongside a public footpath, but there seemed no way in which the currants could be reached without some act of unusual flexibility. The secret was revealed by chance one lunchtime when I noticed a panel of fencing being swivelled to one side and a juvenile hand groped through for a fresh dessert. More for amusement than malice, I lurked by the fence the next day and grasped the hand as it appeared with a maniacal cry that had recently featured in a Dracula re-make. Though everything went into it, my effort was paled by an infinitely more blood-chilling shriek of terror from the other side of the fence, causing me to recoil from the captured hand. I never saw the face that went with it, but no further sorties were made and a new nail solved the problem entirely.

RASPBERRIES

Raspberries, now fabled through rhyming slang as a lewd noise, can in their plant form be an innocent addition to the garden. They are not particularly fussy but do need supporting by a pole and wire framework four to five feet high according to the variety.

Freshly bought canes are planted to a depth of three inches and then cut down to around ten inches above the ground. After the second fruiting, cut old canes down to soil level, keeping half a dozen of the best, new ones. At the end of February the remaining canes can be reduced to six inches above the highest wire.

STRAWBERRIES

One other possibility is strawberries, a great delicacy particularly when home-grown. Raised in open ground they tend to need a lot of attention, so containers are a better bet for the casual gardener.

One very simple method is to raise strawberries in growing bags, which will usually take ten plants. Make holes around the perimeter of the bag by cutting slits in an X formation. This will allow the flaps to be folded back once the plants are inserted to help retain moisture and keep fruit clean. For watering, slit the top of the bag down the centre. The contents will be dry, so give it a good soaking before the plants go in and keep moist at all times.

One infuriating aspect of strawberry-growing is that plants should be de-blossomed in the first spring, if planted late. This is to allow strong root development before energy is diverted to fruit production. But if you are able to introduce summer varieties the previous August this may not be necessary. This type perpetuates itself by sending out runners which will form into new plants. Unless these are needed to fill another bag, they should be cut off. To get new plants, peg the runners into plastic cups or pots filled with compost. Once the plantlet has rooted it can be separated from the parent. After fruiting, remove all old leaves and burn them.

A more ornamental way of growing strawberries is to plant them in an old barrel. This should have two-inch diameter holes drilled all over it and then be filled with a good compost. Plants can be tucked into the holes and set out at the top of the barrel. For a similar means of growing strawberries, buy a container specially made for the purpose from your garden centre. These are generally much narrower than the average barrel and don't require so much compost. One such product is called Ken Muir Tower Pots, made from polypropylene and comprising interlocking tiers. Six tiers will take twelve plants.

ADDING A GREENHOUSE

At this point it is worth pondering the value of a greenhouse. Its use extends beyond vegetables and fruit, usually accommodating salads, and bedding and pot plants. To justify the price of such an aid you have to make it work and not turn it into a transparent shed.

A great range is available, though today the amateur is more often influenced by the aluminium frame type because assembly is easier and structural maintenance minimal.

These come in many shapes and sizes from square ones to oblong ones, domed and round, lean-to and even conservatory. Many can be easily extended at a later stage if more space is needed.

Your aluminium greenhouse kit will arrive in a number of boxes. The only heavy units are those containing glass, and it's surprising how much half-a-dozen sizeable sheets weigh. Unwrapping will reveal a stunning selection of bits, totally un-recognisable. But careful study of the instructions should reveal the function of each and if strictly followed will culminate in a familiar shape. Assembly is not difficult but it may take longer than you anticipate.

One feature that can save time and effort is a steel base, which replaces the otherwise necessary brick foundation. Several manu-facturers offer this as an extra, among them Tropical, and the finished job seems stable enough.

Glazing, the final stage of construction, is an exciting aspect of the job, particularly if, like me, you are totally incompatible with the material. I expect every piece to shatter into a thousand fragments on approach and the actual insertion of holding clips is almost more than I can bear. This is definitely a two-person job and breakages, though not inevitable, cause considerable distress. There are shocking tales of even the most staunch church member loudly broadcasting oaths ancient and modern during a crisis in greenhouse assembly.

Much anguish at the glazing stage can be avoided if you have previously taken care to ensure that the framework is square in all directions. Impatience should not over-ride this vital phase, because it's no good having square pieces of glass to fit a trapezius shaped hole.

Once your greenhouse is completed, the usual thing is to have a central pathway bordered by two beds – for growing things, not sleeping in. These should be filled with good soil and compost. Alternatively you can surface the entire floor area and grow everything in pots and bags.

Accessories are numerous, the first option being some staging, or bench, along one side. An impressive gadget is the automatic roof window opener, solar powered to open and close the vent according to the temperature inside. It's easily fitted and costs around £11. Other bits and pieces like shelves, louvre vents, capillary watering devices etc can be added as your enthusiasm develops.

As far as introducing plants is concerned, tomatoes are easily the most popular. If your greenhouse is heated these can be raised from seed, but bought plants go in during April and May. Their cultivation is almost exactly the same as for outdoor ones. Keep the plants well watered and pinch out the tips when the top of the greenhouse is reached. Because tomatoes are very susceptible to virus infections, they should not be grown in the same soil each year unless it has been sterilised. A change of soil, or growing bags, are the alternatives.

CUCUMBERS

Cucumbers like a more humid atmosphere than tomatoes and so generally do better on their own. But vast numbers of people do grow them together, with fair success, so don't be deterred from buying a couple of plants. They grow very quickly, will need some support and have a sex discrimination problem. Many cucumber plants produce male and female flowers. The male versions must be removed otherwise cucumbers will appear in funny shapes and have a bitter taste. Crippling to the male ego as it is, the simple way out is to buy an all-female variety such as Femspot.

Lettuce can be grown all year round in a heated greenhouse where fifty degrees can be maintained. But even without heating, the extra warmth available extends the normal growing season and plants can be stuck around young tomatoes to make the most use of space.

Radish can be sown in deep trays on the bench and remain where they are, or they can be sown directly into a spare patch of ground within the greenhouse.

Pot plants such as cyclamen, pelargoniums, primulas, fuchsias, cineraria, coleus, begonias, schizanthus and bulbs are good greenhouse subjects to be brought into the house when needed. And considerable money can be saved by raising your own bedding plants from seed, sown in trays of compost kept covered by glass or polythene to maintain a humid environment for germination. A few sheets of newspaper at germination stage will also keep in warmth and stimulate growth. This is removed once the green parts appear.

There is far more to greenhouse gardening than can possibly be included here. Suffice it to say that when used to full effect the benefits are considerable. And if you have trouble justifying it to yourself, remember that conservatories double up to provide extra living space; companies like Florada offer attractive aluminium-framed versions, which once more make basic construction little more than a weekend job.

6. Maintenance & Optional Extras

Though we have tried to keep maintenance down to the minimum, a certain amount will certainly be necessary for tidiness and general benefit of the garden.

WEEDING

Weeding is such a task, and in open areas is best achieved by hoeing when the invaders are still small. In more restricted parts, hand extraction may be necessary. An important thing to remember is that when a weed flowers it will seed, and produce hundreds more like itself. So to ease control, never let garden weeds get this far advanced.

Selective weed killers can also be bought and these are particularly useful for an infected lawn. But be careful what you buy. Some will annihilate every green object in sight and render the soil useless for a while. Make sure that the potion you get is right for the purpose and follow all instructions carefully. And don't use mowings from freshly treated lawns for compost heaps until four cuts have been made.

Flame guns are a spectacular aid, shrivelling weeds and, to some extent, cleaning the upper soil of pests and lurking diseases. They must naturally be used with care otherwise the wrong thing will be blasted or the whole garden go up in flames, certainly too radical a revenge to contemplate.

Something Willie asked me about was the effect of verbal abuse on weeds. There are gardeners who believe that flattering or encouraging conversation with plants will assist their growth. The thing is, would the opposite be damaging to weeds? Here we are up against an ignorance of plant psychology. For example, does a weed think it's beautiful, or does it revel in unpopularity? If the latter is the case then insults might be lapped up, inspiring even more vigorous development.

But assuming weeds are sensitive to criticism, what sort of phrases might be the most devastating, remembering that they must be said aloud and therefore subject to public hearing? You might experiment with the following general purpose sarcasms:

1. 'If all weeds were like you I'd get some more.'
2. 'I've seen better growing in a bag of arsenic.'

3. 'Against you a greenfly would look like the Incredible Hulk.'
4. 'Next door have got a dandelion that's a living legend and I get stuck with a rubbish heap reject.'

If these fail, then consider throwing in a vast insult such as:

'You grotty little object. About as useless as a pair of ballet tights to a bare-back porcupine rider. If they gave medals for first degree pillocks you'd be first in the queue and I'd have you pressed if it wasn't for the fact that the paper would curl up laughing.'

Such a tirade ought at least to cause some drooping if there is any substance in the insult theory. Either that, or the thing will jump out of the ground and bite you. But be especially careful not to use such remarks when they might be overheard by someone who could mistake them for an unprovoked and personal attack on themselves.

Some weeds can be particularly obstinate, needing personal physical attention. Bindweed or twitch is phenomenally resilient and generally has to be attacked at close quarters, pulling out as much root as possible. Small sections left in the ground will re-generate.

Things like dandelions and chickweed can be useful. Full board rabbits, guinea pigs, tortoises and other domestic pets will trough into this sort of weed, as do some people. Personally I still prefer lettuce.

Obstinate dandelions and thistles, which are typical of the weed that has as much if not more below the ground than above, will not usually surrender to tugging. This type has to be dug out to its full subterranean extent if remaining root sections are not to rise Phoenix-like to plague you again. An old knife will often do the job.

LAWN PROBLEMS

Moss in lawns can be a problem, particularly in wet seasons and if drainage is poor. While the temptation is to leave it, since it's green and matches the rest anyway, it will gradually take over from the grass and then spread rapidly. There are any number of proprietary moss killers around which are simply spread over the infected areas. The moss turns brown as it dies off and should be raked out for burning. Small, bare patches will fill in naturally, or you can always scatter a little grass seed to speed your lawn's recovery.

If you want to be fussy, bumps and hollows in lawns can be easily rectified. For small dips, some finely sieved soil added to the top will often do. For more serious depressions the normal practice is to lay back the turf, fill the hollow with soil and then cover it all up again. Bumps are treated in much the same way except in this case soil is removed. When cutting sections of turf, allow a good two inches of thickness to avoid mangling the roots.

The means of cutting lawns has already been discussed, but since the chore is a regular one, perhaps a little more detail in execution is warranted. Frequent mowing does improve the general standard, by controlling the coarser grasses which tend to have a keener interest in growth. Mowing in different directions also helps, particularly if you have a cylinder mower, because the blades are caught at a variety of angles. Also with cylinder mowers, larger stalks of coarse grass survive because they are pushed flat and escape the blades. These can either be pulled out or felled with shears. The problem does not occur with rotary mowers which, because of their action, can deal with much longer material.

The ultimate lawn takes a great amount of maintenance, but among our options would also come feeding. If you were a clump of grass, Sunday roast or sausage and chips would mean nothing. What would really get the old taste buds going would be a dollop of nitrogen, phosphates, potash, calcium, magnesium, iron, manganese, copper and boron. Fortunately this appetising dish does not have to be hand-prepared before serving, any more than you would buy the ingredients to make up a tin of soup. All are found in the appropriate quantities in bags of lawn fertiliser (sometimes with weedkiller included) which is spread evenly over the surface, to be washed in by rain or a hose sprinkling. Manufacturers list the correct helping and life is made much easier by getting a wheeled distributor. They are relatively inexpensive and can also be used for sowing lawn seed.

You will probably find two types of lawn dressing – one for spring and one for autumn. As a rule, the former has a higher nitrogen content for healthy foliage growth and the other has more phosphates and potash to give roots a boost.

QUENCHING THIRST

Watering, just a joke in Britain at times, is still more of a maintenance necessity than an option. It is particularly vital to freshly planted stuff and is best done in the evening when the evaporation rate will be lower. Sprinkling is much the best way, via a hose or watering can. Great tidal waves are not recommended, and over-watering can do more harm than good, apart from being wasteful.

Barrels in which to collect rainwater are well worthwhile, not only in the interest of conserving purified water which in some regions might contain a high and detrimental (to plants) amount of fluoride, but because the natural thing is better and its temperature will be closer to that of the air. As irregular swimmers will know, venturing into water after being baked in the sun can be a great shock to the system. Well, how would you like a bucket of cold liquid thrown over your warm feet? Plants don't think much of it either, particularly in greenhouses. One way of being kind to things growing under glass is to stand a couple of full containers in the greenhouse during the day for application in the evening.

The key to the amount of watering necessary, other than recent great variations in natural deposits, is the type of soil and its ability to hold or get rid of water. Plants need ready access but not excess. As my favourite gardener extraordinary, Geoff Amos, of *Garden News*, so neatly put it (probably towards the end of a liquid lunch): 'It's like keeping a man happy by putting a glass of beer where he can always reach it, but not sickening him by making him stand up to his neck in it.'

The stuff that makes this possible is humus – rotting, waste materials such as manure or compost. So as an option we can improve things for our plants by digging in as much aforesaid humus as possible, because it will lose water through and open up heavy clay soils and retain moisture in and bind together light, sandy soils.

Moisture can also be preserved by mulching, which is a surface dressing of peat mainly applied to flower or shrub borders.

GENERAL FEEDING

As far as general feeding goes, food can be bought in a bottle or packet. Unless inspired to go for a chemical analysis of the soil to detect percentages of elements present, the easy thing is to go for a balanced, compound fertiliser which can be used on just about everything. It is most commonly mixed with water and applied through a can. Everything you need to know will be on the container, and be consoled that it is not an all-year round job, just open to us during the peak growing season.

PRUNING POINTS

Some aspects of pruning have already been mentioned. But it is one of the more emotive subjects in garden maintenance, often incurring heated debates among those experts with strong views. Mostly it is not how but when that promotes the greatest differences of opinion. However, the naive cannot afford to get involved in such disputes and the fact is you will be hard pressed to destroy a plant by pruning provided that certain very basic rules are observed.

Take roses for example, common enough pruning candidates all over the country. Essentially they can be split into four main groups – hybrid teas, floribundas, ramblers and climbers.

Hybrid teas and floribundas are safely pruned in late winter or early spring, as long as frosty periods are avoided. This is because flowers appear on growth produced the same season, so the object is to induce as much new material as possible. Both are taken down to about four buds from the ground the first year after planting. Thereafter they can be reduced to half-length, while dead or diseased wood is taken out altogether. Keep the

centres clear and always cut to outward pointing buds, one eighth of an inch clear and with the separated face sloping down and away. If the cut slopes towards the bud then water will be directed into it, possibly causing rotting. And as a general principle, don't use blunted secateurs or they will crush the stem – and it's damage like this that invites all kinds of plagues.

Ramblers are usually tackled immediately after flowering. They fall into two distinct classes. One type grows new shoots from the base for flowering the following year, and in this case all the old growth is removed. The other one, probably through sheer awkwardness, grows its new material nearer the top. Here the current flowering stems are cut down to a good, strong, new bit and outward growth trimmed back to two or three buds.

Climbers are merely tidied up to stop them sticking up five feet above the fence, and developing into a tangled mass of leaves and thorns.

Two further points remain. One is the removal of suckers, spindly shoots generally quite different from the rest, that appear from the ground in the immediate area of roses. These should not be cut but torn off, even if it means excavating to the main junction. The second useful subsidiary action is to cut off dead flowers, which will assist the development of new ones.

The above is by no means a comprehensive guide to rose butchery, but as elementary principles the instructions should allow a fair degree of passable maintenance.

A certain amount has already been said about fruit trees and bushes, but there is scope for a little pruning work on established apple, plum, pear and cherry trees. Apples and pears get their attention during November and December, consisting primarily of eliminating weak or dead wood and crossing branches. Plums and cherries are polished up in a similar way from late May into early June. For general size control, some summer trimming can be done on all of them; starting from mid-July and throughout August, new extension shoots may be scaled down as required. This often has the secondary effect of promoting fruit buds.

Many shrubs need trimming each year to keep control. Brooms are a typical example, being put to the shears after flowering, as are mature heathers. On the other hand, rhododendrons need never feel the blade, and shouldn't in any case.

In February, provided everything isn't frosted up, clematis that flower before mid-June can be attended to, removing all dead wood and shortening side shoots to the first pair of buds. Later display clematis may have main shoots pruned to a pair of robust buds about three feet from the ground.

POND CARE

If you have a fish pond, this may need topping up during the summer to replace the water lost by evaporation or the dog drinking it. A build-up of algae could turn the water a cloudy green. This is not harmful to fish who, if the truth were known, probably prefer it like that. But since they are not there for their own amusement we can generally deal with the loss of vision by adding a chemical algicide. Dead foliage from plants should be removed.

Little effort is needed in preparing the pool for winter. If a submersible pump is being used, this must either be taken out and cleaned before storing or run for a short while at least once a fortnight to keep it clear of sediment. Many people have a ball floating on the surface in winter to keep a patch free of ice. This is not a breathing hole as many people think – it is to allow any toxic gas build-up from decaying vegetation to escape. Nowadays a small electric pool heater can be floated in the water, using the electricity supply that in summer powers the pump. They use little power because the object is not to warm the entire pool but to keep a small area free of ice. This is only necessary when severe frosts are expected, but always buy the right equipment for the job.

Every three or four years the pool will need cleaning out. The best time to do this is around September, when fish are in peak condition and more able to cope with the traumas of being chased around by a net and confined to plastic buckets until their regular habitat is ready again. Choosing a time of ultimate fitness has its disadvantages. Apart from a basic instinct to avoid being caught, the fish will be that much faster and possibly have more endurance than you. Even the odds a bit by partly emptying the pool first, but despite all frustration remember this is not a Jaws encounter. Spectacular lunges or hand-to-fin grappling can cause grievous injury. The fish might get hurt as well.

7. Squirting

Squirting things is an element of maintenance, but worth a section to itself. Most gardening books give this part the off-putting title of Pests and Diseases, recommending the total war principle of *blitzkrieg*. Many advise on the basis that each offensive will begin by mixing the appropriate spray from its individual ingredients. However it is hardly necessary to act like the local chemist, since just about every potion you're likely to need is readily available, pre-mixed and well labelled as to what doesn't like it. Neither is it essential to attack everything that creeps, hops or crawls in the garden. Certain problems must be treated but others, while perhaps a minor nuisance, need not prompt an 'Earth Wars' spectacular of humanity versus the alien hordes.

GREENFLY
One of the most well-known squirting targets is the greenfly, a member of the aphid family. Easily identifiable, they get on just about everything, assembling in large numbers at the growing tips of plants or in flowers. They feed on sap, causing weakening and dis-

tortion, but are easily controlled. Either buy a spray-gun and the bottle that says 'Greenfly Killer' or, easier still, pick up an aerosol version.

Strangely, aerosol sprays for garden use are still very much of a rarity. There's no doubt you are paying more, but this hasn't stopped the pressurised application of deodorant, domestic flykiller, hair lacquer, anti-perspirants and a multitude of other things. An aerosol for each prime pest and disease would be a tremendous aid to the casual gardener who is more interested in convenience of use rather than economy at the cost of effort.

Because aerosol squirting is so easy compared with mixing a treatment with water in a spray-gun, and then having to wash the container out thoroughly afterwards, it must encourage regular use. Greenfly and the related blackfly can be subdued in this way.

BLACKSPOT AND MILDEW
On roses, blackspot and mildew must be countered. Blackspot is a fungus disease – nothing to do with *Treasure Island*'s Blind

Pugh – which starts in spring on the leaves. Initially the spots are merely specks, but they will increase in size and if left unchecked will cause leaves to drop and generally debilitate the bush. The right mixture, a systemic fungicide, can be bought and is generally squirted on every two weeks between spring and summer. As an extra precaution, tar oil wash can be sprayed on in winter.

Mildew first appears on young leaves as grey spots and will quickly spread over all new growth to retard development. Again the treatment is available in a bottle and can be used from April onwards.

CABBAGE ROOT FLY
Cabbage root fly lays its eggs in the soil around all brassicas (the corporate name for cabbage, cauliflower, sprouts, broccoli etc) and it is hatching larvae or maggots that cause the damage by eating main roots. The symptoms are wilting and a blue colouring, but unless spotted very early it could be too late to prevent serious damage. Better to apply calomel dust around freshly installed plants and/or dust the whole area prior to planting.

CARROT FLY
Carrot fly causes the same sort of problem, with maggots boring into the roots. They are not averse to having a go at parsnips, celery and parsley, either. A sign of such underground vandalism is a reddening of the leaves. Once more it is safest to apply a general soil insecticide before sowing, and add more between the rows during April and May.

FUN WITH FLEA BEETLES
Flea beetles, which attack the foliage of young brassicas, radishes, turnips and swedes, can be fun to catch. As the name implies, they are flea-like and jump. Passing your hand over the tops of plants will produce this activity. While they can be sombrely wiped out by regularly sprinkling the rows of seedlings with derris dust, until the plants are about three inches high, a more cunning method is open to us. Smear grease on an old piece of wood around three inches wide, and then pass this over inhabited plants, making the flea beetles jump. While it would be nice to think that the beetles are stunned by banging their heads on the wood, in fact they only stick to the grease. Such a method is definitely worth a try, having first established the approximate height attainable by an average beetle. This is the kind of technique that makes having a few pests well worthwhile.

CLUB ROOT
Club root is a soil-harboured fungus that picks on brassica roots, causing swelling, splitting and rotting. This offensive disease is best curbed by a sprinkling of calomel dust in the holes made for new plants and changing the location each year. The symptoms are stunting and generally poor growth.

CABBAGE WHITE BUTTERFLY
The infamous cabbage white butterfly is a regular intruder, the hatching caterpillars decimating leaves if left to satisfy their appetites. If you're not squeamish they can be picked off and destroyed, but to avoid physical contact, dust the plants with derris every two weeks from June to September.

SLUGS AND SNAILS
Slugs and snails feed on all kinds of plants, tucking into roots, stems and leaves. A patch of new bedding plants can be eliminated almost overnight by a raid, so protection is essential. The measure is as simple as it is effective, involving the scattering of a few slug pellets, bought by the carton, around known or likely targets. The pellets are naively preferred by the normally indiscriminate slug or snail, and wreak havoc among their numbers. To keep pellets away from pets, place a few under an upturned plant pot, propped up with a stone to allow pest access but not pet access.

Odd snails discovered can be manually

Are there Leprechauns in your Lupins?
Piskies in your Petunia Patch?
Trolls in the Trellis-work?
Hobgoblins in the Hollyhocks?
Nymphs in your Nasturtiums?

Is your Garden a Breeding-Ground
for Elves, Gnomes and Wee Folk?

Exterminate the Tiny Bastards
with

ANTI-SPRITE

disposed of by whatever means you can manage, including throwing them over the fence, or several fences depending on your range and neighbourly relationships – a catapult makes a good snail launcher. This is probably as good a way for a snail to go as any, for one thrilling moment vastly exceeding its normal velocity in free flight. It is also reasonable to assume that if such a disposal system is widely practised, some impact-resistant snails may have travelled miles by air. In the nature of things, a few could well end up where they started from – like back in your garden.

A more recent development is the grandly termed 'non-toxic slug eradicator'. Swiss designers came up with this appealing masterpiece which is a circular, plastic trap, baited, would you believe, with beer! Showing surprisingly human qualities, any slugs within a radius of twenty-five feet can detect the beer and are attracted to it. They crawl up the side, fall in, and are blissfully killed by excessive drinking. Apparently they have no particular preference of brew, but it seems only right to provide best bitter for this final session.

COLORADO BEETLE
As far as potatoes are concerned, blight is probably the most serious problem, other than Colorado beetle – which is a notifiable infestation and relatively rare nowadays. Blight announces itself in the form of brown spots on foliage followed by overall browning and damage to the potatoes themselves. It is advisable to treat this from a precautionary point of view, spraying foliage with Bordeaux Mixture in early July with a booster shot four weeks later. Potato scab might also occur, but this is generally just a blemish on the spud which can be removed during peeling.

WHITEFLY
In a greenhouse, whitefly could be a problem, these being white insects resembling a miniature moth that get together on the underside of leaves. Regular checking will detect the first appearance and squirting with a proprietary whitefly insecticide at around ten-day intervals will ensure that freshly hatched flies are exterminated.

BOTRYTIS
Greenhouse-based tomatoes are also susceptible to Botrytis, a fungus disease that results in a brown tissue on the plant that eventually causes fruit to fall off. It is caused by getting too much water on the lower leaves or too high humidity: so avoiding these will help prevent outbreaks. But in the event spray with some stuff called Cheshunt Compound.

*　　*　　*

With all plants, particularly those that produce something edible, much effort can be saved by checking on their resistance to certain diseases. Tomatoes and potatoes are prime examples because many are able to counter all but the fiercest approach of several common plagues. It is also important not to eat anything that has been recently treated at foliar level. While the effects are not likely to be fatal or even noticeable, it is as well to allow a couple of weeks for the chemical to dissipate.

Larger pests that cannot effectively be dealt with by squirting include birds, moles, worms, cats, dogs and even people.

BIRDS
Birds can be wantonly destructive in removing blossom from trees and more understandably by consuming fruit. Bushes or canes can be protected by plastic netting on a support frame. Frightening devices, either audible or scented, are less predictable, so only experience will tell which methods are effective. My dog chases birds without the remotest chance of ever catching one, but at least they are kept in a nervous state just in case he does.

ANIMALS
Dogs and cats mainly cause damage by clumsiness, by digging, or by relieving themselves on plants. Cat urine can blacken the lower foliage of conifers and kill small

'With farmers blaming birds for destroying £2 million worth of crops in Britain every year, Wurzel and his kind had to go.

Now, electronic robots stand in his place. No fear of missing them: they're all eight feet tall. They have three or four legs and two-foot arms. They wail like banshees and emit blinding flashes of light, which you can see two miles away.

There's been a mobile scarecrow on a tricycle, powered by a lawnmower engine, and a 7ft.-tall tailor's dummy which flapped its arms about.

There's a big plastic hawk on a flexible pole, which hovers and swoops so ominously that they use them at Amsterdam Airport to scare the birds away from the planes.'

from

plants, while that of a bitch is not at all appreciated by lawns. The only way out is to prevent the problem, or, if witnessing it, dilute the scene immediately with water.

MOLES AND WORMS

Moles and worms can infrequently produce blemishes on lawns with their hills and casts. Worm killers are available for application by watering, and this will indirectly deter moles. The reasoning is that moles are only under the lawn to feed on worms: cut off the food supply, and there's not a lot of point worm-stalking in that particular area. It would be like trying to find a copy of *War Cry* at a Satanists' stag night on unlicensed premises in the middle of Romney Marshes, while *Songs of Praise* is on. Difficult.

People, including children, are only a menace while at play, and the sole answers here are careful planning of the garden for a purpose, or a greater degree of discipline than I've ever achieved.

On the whole, the containment of visiting disorders is always best achieved by prevention. A tidy garden has less chance of harbouring unwelcome pests and diseases than one full of rubbish; incorporating deterrents at an early stage can save problems later on; selecting strong healthy plants will ensure them a better chance against natural ravages; while proper aftercare, not too lavish, will further improve their ability to survive.

Inevitably, other problems will come your way. But as in the case of personal physical disorders, all the answers cannot be found in a book, so consult an authoritative source. Publications such as *Garden News* and *Practical Gardening* offer a free advice service for the sake of cutting out a coupon in the current issues. One thing they don't appreciate is a sample insect, alive and well, in the envelope – so make do with a description.

8. Rubbish

A by-product of society – and sometimes an item of direct manufacture – is rubbish. Gardens inevitably produce their share of organic refuse which must be disposed of periodically. There are several ways of doing this. The means can be useful, enjoyable or furtive.

THE BONFIRE

Method one is The Bonfire. There are few more pleasurable jobs in the garden than a ceremonial burning. Great satisfaction can be derived from watching all that unwanted material disappearing in great volumes of smoke, the air enhanced by that distinctive bonfire tang. It is pungently apparent that you are doing something in the garden, and that is definitely good for the new image. Never allow yourself to be seen enjoying the task, however. Always be ready to sympathise with comments about the smoke, and emphasise how happy you will be to see the end of it. Exaggerated coughing and mild oaths can often stifle would-be complainants by arousing pity.

Living with today's 'invisible' domestic heating systems it is easy to forget the great art of lighting fires. Indeed, anyone who has fought to bring a spark of life to some vast, green heap with all the resources of a well-equipped arsonist can be forgiven for wondering how multi-million pound blazes are caused by a carelessly dropped cigarette end. In my experience this technique does not work on things you *want* to burn. Bonfires, in particular, are a challenge.

Here lies the essence of enjoying rubbish disposal by burning. Crisp, dry piles are an exceptional case, presenting no particular difficulty beyond a match applied to a scrap of paper somewhere within the mound. But fresh, wet, green ones ... therein lies a problem to tax the ingenuity and provide some simple amusement.

'Why not wait until the heap has dried out?' you might say. In more predictable climates that might well be valid. But I've had more dry heaps rained on hours before the appointed ignition than I care to remember. There is little more frustrating than such an act of sabotage, so to minimise disappointment it is a good policy to get the thing going at the earliest possible moment.

Most vegetation, no matter how green, will burn given sufficient heat. The secret of the successful green bonfire is to provide that initial catalyst which, in theory at least, creates a chain reaction of drying material to burn to dry more material and so on, and so on.

Fair success can be achieved by screwing up sheets of newspaper – make sure it's not today's – into about half a dozen loose balls. Thrust them into the base of the heap and arrange some dry firewood around and on top of the paper incendiaries. Part of the heap can then be pulled over the arrangement, leaving some paper showing for accepting the light. Your heap should not be too compacted and the principles are not unlike filling a pipe with tobacco – firm but not solid.

After a little practice, individual refinements can be added. A small, empty plastic container, for example, will melt and what's left then burns steadily and for some duration as an aid to building up heat.

Don't be disheartened by a few failures. Look upon bonfire ignition as a skill to be acquired, and avoid the temptation to douse everything in paraffin or some other fuel. That is cheating. It also removes all the enjoyment and probably your hair as well.

A final word, on siting. Obviously you don't start a fifty megaton bonfire close to the house or any other structure that might suddenly become an integral part of it. And don't be carried away by sheer size. It is better to add to the heap, callously selecting which items you will commit to the flames next – like that giant root which took half a day to dig up, or the stinging nettle which just got you in a final gesture of defiance.

THE ROTTING HEAP

Now to our second method of rubbish disposal – The Rotting Heap. This is in no way as entertaining as a bonfire, producing an unsavoury though useful mixture called compost. Such decomposed matter can be returned to the soil as nutrition. Only a plant would appreciate it.

The finished product is at its best when resembling farmyard manure in texture and a dark greenish brown in colour. Faced with some quantity of this vegetable relish, you will be only too pleased to bury it.

It is as well to position the rotting heap out of view as far as is possible. Only the most dedicated will make it a proud feature of their garden. The principles are extremely simple, nevertheless, and the horticultural values indisputable.

Rotting heaps are built in layers, say ten inches of rubbish covered with an inch of soil, and so on. You don't need a ruler to measure the depths because they aren't that critical. All that's happening is that bacteria in the soil starts to attack your rubbish, breaking down the structure into a more concentrated and re-usable form. The heap will decrease in size as this happens, meaning you can put more on it.

Virtually any green stuff can be added, but there's little point in donating woody bits which will take years to disappear. Generally six months is enough, though there are special activators you can buy to speed things up and even devices that enable you to own a 'canned' heap, working like a little factory. Definitely a possibility for one-upmanship, and tidier too.

Without going into organic chemistry, which hardly anyone understands anyway, and boring you with such terms as *pH values* and *calcareous* soils, that is all you need to know. We must at all times maintain a certain level of ignorance.

THE DUSTBIN

Right. Hands up those who put garden rubbish in the dustbin. So do I.

This is often a furtive method of disposal, stuffing empty cornflake boxes with weeds or some other ingenious means of disguise. Blatantly crowning your bin or bins with half a tree or some unappetising refuse is not good practice and will only antagonise the dustman. Whatever the ethics, it is essential to stay on good terms with him and this requires a reasonable approach plus a generous tip at Christmas.

Unless you are using the rotting heap method, grass cuttings can present the greatest difficulty of disposal. Given a good relationship with the dustman, these will often be taken away if neatly packed in a tied polythene sack. Don't keep it lying around too long, however, because grass cuttings become rather putrid and no one, but no one, is going to touch such a puke-provoking package with a bargepole.

Be prepared to cut up twigs and other largish objects into smaller sizes so that they might filter into the normal household refuse. I have successfully disposed of an old double mattress via the dustbin by breaking it down into its component parts. A radical and time-consuming scheme, but needs find a way. The object, however, is not to deceive the collector of bins, one of today's most under-rated public employees (crawler!), but to utilise further an existing service by presenting unclassified rubbish in an acceptable way.

Perhaps the ultimate extension of this approach, though I've never tried it, is to fill a large cardboard box with rubbish, gift wrap it complete with bow and greetings label, then leave it on the back seat of your unlocked car in a vehicle park. With any luck, someone might pinch it. The risk is they might take the car as well.

THE TIP

One more possibility remains. That is to take the rubbish to a nearby tip. Some local authorities permit this free of charge, some accept a small fee, and others provide one of those large hoppers resembling a truncated landing craft at some central point, to accept large items.

Don't just throw rubbish in the nearest hedge on a midnight expedition. An unemployed gardener might be sleeping there.

9. Finding Something To Do

Without doubt, this is the best part of the book – finding something to do outside after The Thing has been finally sedated to a more obedient level.

Stationary occupation is a start. This can involve sitting, lying down or swinging. Standing up is also a possibility but nowhere near as popular. For this range of inactivity you will need some garden furniture and there are vast possibilities.

SEATING

Collapsing chairs are best if storage is a problem. They can also be easily transported in the car for days out, and are light enough to carry on treks across beaches looking for vacant sites. Some are not particularly robust, those incorporating fabric support being prone to unexpected collapsing. This does bring great joy to observers if nothing else.

The most extreme case I can recall involved some tubular-framed chairs pressed into service for a canteen. They were so badly constructed that barely a day passed without one folding up under its occupant. Canteen breaks became periods of intolerable tension, as everybody eagerly awaited the fate of someone else and willed his or her own chair to stay in one piece. The enraptured silence was broken only by the anticipated event. A sharp crack of fractured welds was the only advance warning, by which time it was far too late to make any sort of recovery. All eyes swung to the sound, generally just in time to see the unfortunate's rapid descent, often with a cup of coffee still suspended in mid-air. The moral of that story is to buy the best you can afford, and prices do vary dramatically for very similar items.

One thing that always seems to exude the principle of leisure is a patio set, usually comprising a sunshade, table and chairs. This has to be a priority purchase for the optimist, who is resolute in the belief that shade will be necessary at some time or another. The sunshade goes through a hole in the centre of the table to be anchored in a sand or water-filled base supplied. Most shades can also be stuck in grass or sand to extend their usefulness.

Decadent reclining chairs or sun loungers are excellent aids to laziness while more formal wooden seats and tables can be bought for permanent siting outside.

SWINGING

Modest swinging can be achieved in a hammock. Nowadays you don't need two convenient trees for attachment, as self-contained hammocks with frames are obtainable. The frame is quickly assembled and dismantled for storage. Swinging is limited, except when getting in and out, a risky operation until the technique is mastered. Once you are centrally placed, only energetic action will make your hammock move substantially; though a slumbering roll to one side or embarkation of a second party, like the dog, can bring instant awareness of the precarious suspension. As a rule, the only casualties are novices or victims of circumstance, sometimes premeditated.

The ultimate aid to garden decadence is the swinging lounger, complete with frilled canopy. Though still sadly beyond my experience, I can well imagine the tranquillity of temper and paralysis of purpose such a device would provide. It's about as far removed from a towel on the lawn as a thermal lance from a sharp stick.

GAMES

So much for idleness. What if you are moved to some form of recreation other than eating and drinking? A great number of ball games can be played in the garden, its size being the only major restriction. It is not usually feasible to undertake five-a-side football matches, polo, cricket, tennis etc, but more modest games abound.

For the small garden, Swingball is one of the most suitable. If you are unfamiliar with the equipment, essentially it consists of a tennis ball on the end of a cord which in turn is attached to a great spring on top of a pole. Two players beat the ball about, the winner being the one who can reach the top or bottom of the spring according to which way you're hitting. Apart from being struck round the ear by a missed ball, little else disastrous can happen other than the cord separating – in which case its ultimate destination is in the

lap of the gods. This game is definitely suitable for confined spaces, and will provoke keen competition if not a killer instinct. You can also do it alone when no one else will play.

Less energetic is the French game of boules. This is a sort of variation on green bowling, the object being to place balls closest to a target. They can be rolled or cast and an uneven surface merely adds to the degree of difficulty, or pure luck. Disputes can arise as to who has the closer ball and having a hitherto winning shot blasted out of sight by an enemy fluke strains sportsmanship to the limit. 'Oh, what a demon ball, well done', you say nobly while thinking: 'You lucky (*expletive of choice*). The (*second choice expletive*) thing slipped out of your hand.'

Cheap croquet sets pass away the time on a lawn without significant effort, while restrained badminton is not too bad and a misdirected shuttlecock can't do much damage. Open air darts might appeal – hang the board on a convenient fence/wall/garage; actual or phantom gusts of wind can be blamed for minor inaccuracies, and there's always the chance that a desperately unlucky fly might be impaled for a bonus score. Make sure there is no risk of a wildly misdirected arrow escaping to a region where it could cause injury. (With some players I know, the safest place to be is directly in front of the board.)

Stilt walking is certainly less common, but in the interests of child amusement and looking over next door's fence, an obstacle course might be laid out. For extra interest try poking the stilts down your trouser legs; it's amazing how a sense of balance is heightened by the necessity for self-preservation. On second thoughts, I shouldn't bother.

The spotting and annihilation of individual ants can effortlessly occupy the mind for some time, though the ethics are a little worrying. For some reason it seems acceptable to attack ants en masse but not separately. I'm sure it must have something to do with the impersonal development of more serious conflict. It isn't that long since Trafalgar, when one of the most embarrassing moments was the arrival of a British

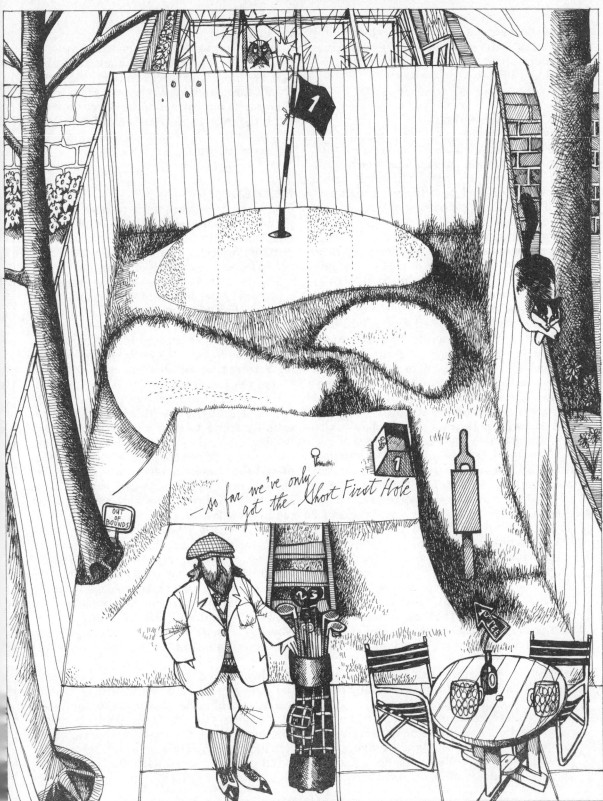

—so far we've only got the Short First Hole

officer on a stricken enemy ship which hadn't actually surrendered. After profuse apologies, he returned to continue the bombardment. Those were the days!

SWIMMING POOLS

It is just possible that you might have considered some means of partial or total immersion for the garden. Children's paddling pools are no problem, being either inflated or erected on a frame as required. Adults, too, can find some comfort on a hot day by wading through them.

Something more ambitious can be an expensive item. The cheapest form of actual swimming-pool is an above the ground one. These generally start at twelve-foot diameter circles, moving up to more oblong shapes large enough to make a few strokes in. Such a pool is simply constructed, being laid on a sand base with a liner to hold the water within steel walling. If you are contemplating buying a pool, go for the largest you can accommodate or afford. Smaller ones require just as much equipment and maintenance as their larger cousins, so it's as well to go the whole hog as mess about with something that is just a generous bath.

Essential extras would include a pump/filter, all the necessary chemicals plus a water testing kit, a surface skimmer to take off floating leaves and insects and, in my experience, an underwater suction cleaner for getting out submerged material which otherwise has to be painstakingly netted.

Unfortunately, it is the unpredictable English summer that influences pool purchase. As a proud new owner you may be encouraged to get full value for money by plunging in on even the most fresh days, but that is a novelty that soon passes. For about as much money again, a plastic dome can be added to your pool, which does extend the season and keep out those breezes diplomatically described as 'bracing'. But whatever you do, an above the ground pool is bound to lose heat more rapidly than one fully installed, thereby being relatively cold compared with the evening air temperature. An in-ground pool often presents a favourable warmth against the air level because of the insulation properties.

Don't be put off though. The cost of a modest pool can soon be balanced against savings in regular weekend motoring to the coast, apart from all the aggravation which that particular form of masochism involves. It all depends on resources and inclination, plus some decent weather to make the whole project worthwhile.

BARBECUES

One of the most pleasant aspects of a leisure garden is the barbecue. This doesn't have to be a lavish orgy of eating and drinking; just as much fun can be gained from a few bacon sandwiches, beefburgers or sausages.

The choice of barbecue equipment is fairly comprehensive, basically comprising those that are brought out as needed and others that are built in as a permanent feature. The portable variety comes in many shapes and sizes, some featuring a battery-powered spit for rotating small chickens and whatever else can be skewered.

Barbecues are powered by charcoal, which has to be brought to a glowing red before it actually starts to cook anything. Firewood, firelighters and assorted inflammables are used to bring about this state which is preceded by smoke clouds, blowing, coughing and encouraging/threatening words. It is advisable to bring the barbecue to peak condition before any guests arrive.

It is a widely held belief that barbecued meats have a distinct flavour. This may well be true, although my own ruined palate cannot honestly detect a vast difference between them and those cooked by more conventional means. For this reason I am prone to cheating, that is using a gas-powered camping cooker for impromptu 'barbecue' sessions. After all, who could arrange an evening of savage cooking even a few days ahead with any great confidence that the appointed evening will be climatically suitable? So, if you have the alternative gear, there's little point in going specialist except for the atmosphere, which certainly is distinctive.

What really helps a barbecue, of whatever proportion, is artificial lighting. Britain lags

behind many parts of Europe in this area, but it really does extend your environment during darkness. It can be permanently built into a garden and companies such as Emess Lighting produce a considerable number of weatherproof varieties. The most effective colours are green and amber, when these are used in conjunction with foliage. But clear illumination for patios is a surer way of checking on the effect your food is having, and also seeing that no one is secretly throwing it away.

A commendable philosophy is that the garden is an extension of the home and vice versa. Essentially such a principle campaigns for the maximum use of available space. Once The Thing Outside has been tamed, other opportunities for use often present themselves. So while the main battle might end here, the art of living with and enjoying your garden fully is a subject that's only just beginning.

ARE WE ABOUT TO IMITATE THE ACTIONS OF THE LEMMING, SIR, OR PLOUGHING THE FIELDS AND SCATTERING?

10. Glossary

Knowledgeable gardeners have their own language, and might just as well be speaking in a foreign tongue as far as most of us are concerned. While you will undoubtedly be able to make out the odd word – usually one emphasising the nuisance value of a particular cat or pestilence – the following selection of terms and expressions should give you a fuller understanding of what is being said.

Try to memorise the list, and then practise words in conversation with those more fluent. Start with simple phrases such as 'My brassicas have bolted' or 'There are no flies on my herbaceous perennials'.

That first glimmer of understanding that shows you have successfully communicated with another race is a wonderful moment, and will continue to give great pleasure as your vocabulary increases.

Activator: A substance which provides the fuel for bacteria to start the rotting down process in compost heaps.

Algae: Minute plants that cause green slime in pools or on paths.

Annual: A plant that flowers in one season from seed and then dies.

Arbor: A rustic structure around which climbing plants are grown, generally roses.

Axil: The angle between leaf and stem from which ancillary buds develop.

Ballast: A mixture of sharp sand and gravel for making concrete.

Bark-ringing: The removal of small strips of bark to reduce vigour and increase productivity, mainly for fruit trees.

Bi-annual: A plant that flowers in two years and then dies.

Blanching: Covering stems with soil or opaque material to exclude sunlight and produce white stems (celery, chicory etc).

Bolting: When plant runs to seed, often due to dry weather.

Bolster: A wide metal chisel for cutting stone or bricks.

Brassicas: Collective name given to greens, such as cabbage and cauliflower.

Budding: A method of propagation used to join the bud of one plant to the stem of another.

Chitting: The pre-germination of seed before sowing, a method often applied to potatoes.

Cloche: French for 'bell' – a glass or plastic structure for producing early crops and protecting from frost.

Cold Frame: A small, rigid glass or plastic structure used for hardening-off young plants or growing protected crops.

Compost: Rotted-down organic matter, used to improve soil quality.

Composts: Media for sowing and potting.

Concrete: A mixture of sand, gravel, cement and water.

Coniferous: A cone-bearing plant.

Contact chemical: An insecticide, fungicide or weedkiller that is effective when in contact with the pest.

Container growing: A modern nurseryman's method of growing plants for sale. The plant will have spent all its life in a container.

Consolidate: To firm the ground.

Cordon: An intensive form of training plants, mainly fruit trees.

Cultivar: A variety of plant produced by man by breeding.

Cutting: A shoot, generally with a growing point, used as a means of propagation.

Dead-heading: The removal of blooms, once they have started to die, to prevent plants making seed.

Deciduous: A plant that loses its leaves in winter.

Disbudding: Reducing the number of buds on a stem in order to increase the size of flower or fruit.

Drills: Small furrows in which to place seeds.

Earthing up: The process of banking soil against the stems of plants in order to exclude sunlight or provide support.

Espalier: An intensive method of training fruit trees against a wall in horizontal tiers; can refer to the lattice-work of wood on which the trees are trained.

Evergreen: A plant that keeps its leaves winter and summer.

Fans: An intensive method of training plants against walls, particularly fruit trees.

F1 hybrid: A vigorous hybrid produced by crossing two specific varieties. Seeds saved from F1 hybrids will not produce plants like the parent.

Floret: Small individual flowers making up a flower head.

Foliar feeding: Applying fertiliser to the leaves to be absorbed there rather than by the roots.

Fruit bud: A bud that will produce fruit.

Fruitlet: A small fruit.

Germination: The first visible signs of a seed turning into a plant.

Grafting: A method of propagating plants, particularly trees, by joining a stem of one to the roots of another.

Growth bud: A bud that will produce a stem.

Half-hardy: A plant that requires greenhouse protection until all danger of frost has gone.

Hardy: A plant that will stand temperatures below freezing.

Hardcore: Coarse rubble used in foundation work.

Hardening off: The process of gradually acclimatising plants raised in a warm greenhouse to colder conditions outside.

Haulm: The top growth of some plants, particularly potatoes.

Herbaceous: Plants with soft stems.

Herbaceous perennials: Herbaceous plants that die down to the ground naturally.

Hormone: A substance used to affect growth. In weedkillers it accelerates growth to an intolerable level, killing the plant.

Hybrid: A cross between two varieties to combine the desired qualities of each.

Hydroponics: The practice of growing plants in a nutrient solution without soil.

Indigenous: Native to a particular country.

June Drop: Natural thinning of fruits when the tree is carrying too many to produce a reasonable amount of seed.

Layering: A method of plant propagation by inducing roots to grow from a cut stem plunged into soil.

Leggy: Spindly growth, usually the result of lack of light.

Loam: A term generally used to denote good, fibrous soil, often used in potting composts.

Mortar: A mixture of soft sand, cement and water used mainly in bricklaying.

Mulching: Spreading organic matter around plants to reduce moisture loss through evaporation, or to shade roots.

Node: The point where the leaf joins a stem.

Non-residual: A term used in connection with weedkillers, indicating that the chemical is rapidly broken down after use and neutralised.

Organic: Anything that is, or was, alive.

Peat: Remains of vegetation that has decayed in bog conditions. Used in composts and as a soil conditioner.

Perennial: A plant that continues to grow seasonally until it dies of old age or disease.

pH: The unit of measurement of acidity or alkalinity (of soil or water in garden use).

Plasticiser: An additive for concrete or cement, which makes the substance easier to work.

Plunging: Placing pots up to their rims in soil, ashes or peat or similar material to help prevent drying out.

Pointing: Filling joints between bricks, stonework or paving with mortar.

Pollination: Fertilisation of female flowers by male flowers by deposit of pollen.

Potting off: Putting a young plant into its first pot.

Potting on: Transferring a plant from its present pot to the next size up.

Pricking out: Transferring seedlings from one seed tray to another, or to a pot, in order to space them out.

Propagation: Increasing plants by seed, cuttings, or layering.

Puddling-in: Soaking soil around the roots of a newly introduced plant.

Pyramids: An intensive form of training small fruit bushes.

Riddle: A sieve for grading.

Rootcrop: A crop grown for its edible roots, such as potatoes and carrots.

Rooting powder: A powder containing the hormones which activate rooting. Used when taking cuttings.

Rootstock: A plant specially bred to control root vigour of plants that are to be grafted on to it.

Runners: Small plants produced on long, root-like stems.

Scalping: Cutting a lawn so short so that the grass roots are exposed.

Scorching: The killing of leaf and stem tissue by too much sunlight or wind.

Seedling: A recently germinated plant.

Side-shooting: Removing side growths from the main stem of a plant to concentrate vigour.

Shuttering: Wooden formers used to retain concrete.

Spiking: Making holes (mainly in lawns) to allow entry of air and water.

Spores: 'Seeds' of non-flowering plants like ferns and mosses.

Sport: Bloom of a different colour or form arising from a plant, caused by a genetical mix-up.

Staging: Bench arrangement in a greenhouse.

Staking: Supporting a young plant until established.

Stool: The root system of perennial plants, often kept over winter to produce cuttings in spring.

Sucker: Unwanted growth from a rootstock.

Sward: An expanse of grass.

Systemic: Description of chemical taken into the system of a plant through the leaves.

Tender: A plant that will be damaged by low temperatures.

Ties: Objects by which plants are attached to supports.

Top dressing: Spreading organic matter and fertiliser to feed lawns or improve soil structure.

Trace elements: Plant nutrients needed in minute quantities, such as magnesium, iron, calcium.

Truss: A bunch of fruit.

Union: The point of grafting or budding.

Index

127